GEN AI

HOW TO FUTURE PROOF YOUR CHILD

VANESSA & DARREN GRAY

Copyright © 2025 Alliance Health P/L and Vanessa & Darren Gray

All rights reserved.

No part of this publication may be reproduced, stored in a retrieval system, or transmitted in any form or by any means — electronic, mechanical, photocopying, recording, or otherwise — without prior written permission of the publishers, except in the case of brief quotations embodied in critical articles or reviews.

Independently published via Amazon Kindle Direct Publishing

ISBN: 978-1-7644414-0-7

Cover design by Naureen Wazir

Illustrator: Nishat Zahan

Disclaimer

This book is intended for informational and inspirational purposes only. The authors are educators, not medical or legal professionals.

Dr Darren J. Gray is an AHPRA-registered chiropractor in New South Wales, Australia, using the courtesy title "Dr" as permitted. He is not medically trained or registered as a medical practitioner. The ideas and information in this book — whether clinical, research, or theoretical — are based on current science but do not constitute medical advice or the opinion of a neurologist.

Readers are encouraged to seek independent guidance from a qualified medical doctor or neurologist before beginning any treatment or relying on this information. The authors and publisher disclaim any liability arising directly or indirectly from the use of material contained in this book.

All classroom stories, teaching examples, and student references in this book are anonymised composites drawn from the authors' professional teaching experiences. Identifying details such as names, ages, genders, school locations, and other personal characteristics have been altered, generalised, or omitted entirely to protect student privacy and confidentiality.

Where public figures are mentioned, references are included only in a factual, biographical, or inspirational context. These individuals have not endorsed, authorised, or contributed to the contents of this book. Any opinions, interpretations, or reflections are solely those of the authors.

The authors' reflections on classroom practice are provided in a personal capacity and do not necessarily represent the policies, views, or practices of their current or past employers. The authors have made every effort to ensure that examples comply with professional, ethical, and legal standards in education.

The copyright for all original text, reflections, and professional practice commentary remains the property of the authors. No part of this book may be reproduced, distributed, or transmitted in any form without prior written permission, except in the case of brief quotations used in reviews or academic discussion.

For permissions or enquiries, contact: genai@brainstormrehab.com.au

First Edition: 2025

TABLE OF CONTENTS

Foreword 8

Second Foreword 14

Preface: Why We Wrote This Book 19

About the Authors 26

INTRODUCTION: EMBRACING THE NEW WORLD OF LEARNING 30

Overview 31

PART ONE: OVERWHELMED 40

Chapter 1: The Truth About Modern Learning 41

Chapter 2: Gamer Minds – Turning Play Into Purpose 56

Chapter 3: Rethinking Success – Skills for a Changing World 76

PART TWO: UNDERSTOOD 93

Chapter 4: Building a Growth Mindset in an AI World 94

Chapter 5: The Parent-Child Learning Partnership ... 117

Chapter 6: Technology and AI in Learning 134

PART THREE: EQUIPPED 170

Chapter 7: Beyond the Glass Ceiling — Her Turn 171

Chapter 8: What Schools Can Do (And Can't Do) 184

Chapter 9: Student Voice in the Age of Gen AI 196

Chapter 10: The Power of Play and Creativity 207

Chapter 11: Raising Independent Learners 219

Chapter 12: The Art of Letting Go 240

Chapter 13: Guardrails Not Gatekeepers 259

Chapter 14: The New Grandparenting – Co-Parents, Not Just Carers 278

PART FOUR: DIFFERENT MINDS, SAME FUTURE 302

Chapter 15: Wired Differently – AI and Children With Learning Differences 303

Chapter 16: High-Voltage Hearts, High-Speed Minds 334

PART FIVE: TAKING ACTION 352

Chapter 17: Empowering Your Home With AI 353

Chapter 18: Navigating the Future Together 377

Bibliography 396

Epilogue: A Legacy of Curiosity 425

FOREWORD

By Dr Nici Sweaney

We're at a crossroads, and we're the last generation that gets to decide which way we go.

Education has been part of my DNA since I was young. My dad was a teacher, then a high school principal, and watching him work instilled in me just how important education really is - I genuinely believe it's the single most powerful force shaping both individual lives and our collective future. My partner is a primary school teacher today, so conversations about learning and student outcomes remain part of our daily rhythm. But even beyond these family connections, I've always been deeply committed to educational equity - ensuring every child has genuine opportunities to succeed, regardless of their starting circumstances.

That foundation led me into science, then data science, and eventually into my current work as a global advocate for ethical AI implementation in education and business. I've delivered over a hundred keynote presentations, advised thousands of individuals and organisations, and collaborated with educators and policymakers across continents on AI strategy and policy. As a parent to four children aged 4 to 12, these aren't just professional pursuits for me - they're deeply personal ones too.

Here's the fundamental truth I return to in every conversation: AI is neither inherently good nor bad. It is simply extraordinarily powerful. And right now, we all represent the only generation of adults who will ever have the opportunity to shape how it enters our children's lives.

This reality terrifies some people, and I understand why. The headlines sound dystopian. We're all exhausted from trying to keep up with the ever changing digital landscape, and now there's a whole new beast to deal with. But regardless of how you feel about AI and children - one thing is for sure - our kids will encounter, and use, AI whether we guide them to or not. The question isn't whether they'll use it - it's whether we'll be part of that conversation.

And we have to be. Because I wholeheartedly believe that some amazing 15-year-old is going to use AI to solve climate change or cure diseases in ways our adult brains could never imagine. But that's only going to happen if we give them the right foundation - if we talk to them about ethics and creativity and the importance of their own thinking, and if we help them navigate all the tricky safety issues that come with this technology.

That's why I'm so excited about what Vanessa and Darren have created here. They haven't just written another parenting guide or education manual - they've created something genuinely brave.

They're willing to say what needs to be said: that we can't just panic and ban everything, but we also can't just hope for the best. We need guardrails, not gatekeepers.

We need to be partners with our kids in figuring this out together.

What I love about Vanessa and Darren's approach is how they really see children - not as fragile beings who need protecting from everything, but as resilient, curious humans who deserve honest conversations and good guidance. They understand that inaction is worse than messy action. They show us how to scaffold opportunities for our kids while teaching them to think critically and ethically about these powerful tools.

This book speaks to both parents and educators because it recognises we're all in this together. Whether you're sitting around the dinner table or standing at the front of a classroom, you're facing the same fundamental challenge: how do we prepare children for a world that's changing faster than we can keep up with?

Vanessa and Darren cover everything from the neuroscience of how kids learn to practical strategies for different learning styles to what schools can and can't do right now. They tackle the big philosophical questions about growth mindset and student voice, but they also give you concrete tools for tomorrow's conversations. It's not just theory - it's a roadmap for families and educators who want to engage rather than retreat.

The chapter on "Guardrails not Gatekeepers" alone is worth the price of admission. It perfectly captures what we need to be doing - not locking technology away from our children, but teaching them how to use it thoughtfully and safely.

We have a moral responsibility to our children and our students to get this right. Not perfect - none of us will get it perfect - but right enough that they can take it from here and build something beautiful - better than we could ever imagine. We're the only cohort that gets to influence how AI shapes the next generation's education and opportunities. That's both terrifying and extraordinary. This is an opportunity that I want you to take very seriously.

This book gives us the tools to start that work. It offers hope where there's been fear, practical guidance where there's been confusion, and partnership where there's been isolation.

Our children are counting on us to figure this out. Vanessa and Darren have given us an excellent place to begin.

Dr. Nici Sweaney

BSc, Hons, PhD

Founder & CEO, AI Her Way

Senior Fellow, AI for Developing Countries Forum

Australian AI Awards 2025, Female AI Leader of the Year

Finalist, Australian AI Awards 2025 AI Leader of the year

Forbes Women Issue, 2025

SECOND FOREWORD

By Assoc Professor Peter Tuchin (Ret)

I have known Darren Gray for more than 30 years. Initially, I met Darren as a chiropractic student when I was teaching at Macquarie University, and then after graduation, Darren worked with me as an associate in our Gosford practice. Darren had an insatiable thirst for knowledge, and importantly, how to translate knowledge into helping people achieve better health.

Vanessa's background and personal journey provide the perfect opportunity to explore child development, and integrate her experiences with new approaches to supporting children's growth.

Vanessa and Darren's book "AI- How To Future-Proof Your Child" provides, not only their personal insight and stories about their family, but also includes evidence-based knowledge, with the research that supports their ideas.

Vanessa and Darren have a unique perspective, based on their individual knowledge and achievements, but then their combined approach as parents to help their children develop.

The opening sections set the stage by clarifying the importance of new learning approaches or styles of education, combined with use of modern technology, and how this can shape personal and educational perspectives.

They then challenge traditional approaches to learning and introduce new ideas and concepts. These new approaches are explained in detail, and supported by narrative examples. Their material highlights the importance of grounding knowledge in clear, practical and appropriate language.

Integrating theory to practice, their book presents methods, strategies, and tools. Readers are encouraged to apply ideas directly to their own lives or work, and especially in supporting your children's development. Vanessa and Darren's book blends instruction with self-reflection, helping readers see how new ideas translate into tangible steps.

Vanessa and Darren provide a deep layer of analysis on traditional education, and explore the challenges of implementing these ideas in everyday life. They acknowledge obstacles, offering practical ways to overcome them. The tone is motivating and supportive, reinforcing resilience and adaptability.

The final sections pull earlier ideas together into a holistic framework. Patterns and lessons are woven into a coherent message that emphasizes continuity of growth beyond the book itself.

Practical Messages

- Growth requires both knowledge and action: understanding concepts is only half the journey; applying them is transformative.
- Reflection is a critical tool: consistent self-examination fosters clarity and direction.

- Practical strategies succeed when adapted: flexibility ensures that guidance remains relevant across situations.
- Sustained learning leads to empowerment: the book encourages readers to keep developing after the final page.
- Integration is key: lessons must be connected and synthesized, not left as isolated pieces.

Summary

Vanessa and Darren's book is a well-written, reflective and instructional guide designed to provide readers with their personal experiences, research and practical tools for helping children grow. It provides foundational background, core ideas, and real-world applications, which ends with practical solutions.

Their book provides not only information but also a pathway for turning ideas or theories into practice. Its value lies in guiding the reader from awareness to application, and ultimately toward a more empowered and intentional approach to improving your child's life and learning skills.

Assoc Professor Peter Tuchin (Ret)

BSc GradDipChiro DipOHS PhD FACC

Past President, Chiropractic and Osteopathic College of Australasia

Director, Lifeline Harbour to Hawkesbury Sydney

Women's Resilience Centre -Social Impact Committee member

World Federation of Chiropractic, Disability and Rehabilitation Committee member

PREFACE:
WHY WE WROTE THIS BOOK

This book was born out of both deep conviction and lived experience.

As one of just 1,200 educators across Australia to be awarded Highly Accomplished Lead Teacher (HALT) status—a distinction held by less than 1% of teachers nationwide—I've spent my career committed to evidence-based, future-focused education. HALT accreditation is a rigorous, nationally certified process recognising expert teaching practice and sustained impact. It's about more than classroom performance—it's about leadership, mentoring, and driving innovation in learning. I bring that same level of intentionality and integrity to this book.

But my story doesn't begin in the classroom.

I grew up in Tasmania with an active, ocean-centred childhood. My grandfather had been a clearance diver in the Navy, so swimming was non-negotiable — I was in the icy waters of Tasmania before most kids my age could manage a few strokes. With my mum and sister, surf lifesaving became our way of life. Mum went on to become the first female state president of a surf lifesaving club, while the three of us also poured our energy into running a local calisthenics club, where movement and performance nurtured my love of creative expression. Meanwhile, my Dad, he drove trucks for Cadbury and couldn't swim a stroke — he often laughed that even the bathtub was

too deep for him, so he stuck to showers. Away from the water, he was usually behind the curtain of a theatre, working on set design and stage management. Between the surf, the stage, and the calisthenics hall, I learned early that movement, creativity, and resilience were ways of being.

There wasn't a sport I didn't try. Touch football became a passion, and I eventually earned a Queensland scholarship, representing multiple times before transferring north to finish my Physical Education degree. Teaching didn't come easily at first—I worked in gyms, ran personal training sessions before personal training was even a recognised industry, and then took off to Japan to teach English, disillusioned with my future. There, I also worked alongside a doctor of nutrition, preparing him for symposiums around the world. When I came back, I decided to try teaching again. This time it stuck.

I landed in Mackay, Queensland, and through the sport of triathlon I met Darren. From there, our paths began to intertwine—in sport, in family, and in professional life. In 2000 we moved to Port Macquarie, NSW so Darren could establish his first private practice. It was a leap of faith: we arrived at a commercial rental in need of major renovations, in a pre-GST, pre-Sydney Olympics building boom when builders were impossible to find. I started teaching in the Catholic Education system two days after we arrived, and from that moment I knew I had found my professional home. Over time, I moved from Physical Education (PE) into teaching languages (LOTE) and religion (RE). At first, moving away from teaching sports with PE was like giving up my identity. However, I have since discovered a love for helping a student to embrace new cultures, new ideas and different ways of seeing the world.

At the same time, Darren was walking his own path.

In 2007, during the stressful period of relocating our practice, Darren's health suddenly and frighteningly unravelled. What began as a vague sense of exhaustion quickly escalated into something far more alarming. He lost his swallowing reflex, his vision split into double, and numbness crept steadily down one side of his body. Within days, his body seemed to collapse under the pressure, and he was admitted to the hospital.

There, after urgent testing, came the devastating words: Multiple Sclerosis (MS). We had not prepared for this, nor could we have imagined it. In that moment, it felt as though the ground gave way beneath us. The diagnosis carried the shadow of progressive disability, of uncertainty, of an unknown and frightening decline. We were stunned — grieving, bewildered — and left to ask the question no one could answer: what will our future look like now?

Yet, only weeks later, further neurological scans and assessments told a different story. Darren had a scar on his brain, but not the multiple lesions required for MS. Relief washed over us, but it was mixed with frustration, exhaustion, and lingering symptoms that made recovery slow and uncertain.

Still searching for clarity, we flew to Melbourne, Victoria to see a clinical functional neurological practitioner. That meeting changed everything. In the consultation, Darren encountered a radically different perspective — one that challenged the idea of the brain as fragile and inevitably declining. Instead, he was introduced to the science of neuroplasticity, which describes the brain's ability to adapt, rewire, and heal under the right conditions.

That single insight proved transformative. It reframed his illness not as the end of his capacity, but as the beginning of a new direction. From that point on, Darren's professional journey took on a deeper purpose. What began as a terrifying health crisis, became the turning point that inspired his lifelong passion for brain-based neurology and rehabilitation.

That's why I didn't write this book alone.

My husband, Dr. Darren Gray (Chiropractor and Rehab Therapist), co-authored this work with a perspective that is both personal and professional. Darren is not a medical doctor but holds a Bachelor of Science, a Master of Chiropractic and Clinical Rehabilitative

Neurology. With over 35 years of clinical experience, he brings a specialised focus on how the brain learns, adapts, and recovers.

Together, we offer a unique fusion of educational leadership and applied neuroscience. As early adopters rather than sceptics, we believe the real question is not

"Should children use AI?" but— "How can we help them use it wisely, ethically, and with purpose?"

This book is for families who want to stay connected in a time of rapid educational change. It's for parents who want to raise curious, emotionally intelligent, and resilient children—even when the terrain feels unfamiliar. It's for educators who want to honour best practice while preparing students for a world shaped by technology.

This isn't a manual filled with jargon. It's a hopeful, practical roadmap grounded in neuroscience, education, and everyday parenting. It's filled with stories, strategies, and insights—designed to help you raise good humans in an AI-powered world.

We wrote it not because we have all the answers— But because we're walking this journey too.

Let's step into the future—together.

ABOUT THE AUTHORS

Dr. Darren Gray BSc.,MChiro.,MClinRehabNeuro.

Dr. Darren Gray, BSc, MChiro, MClinRehab (Neurology), FAFN is a chiropractor and certified neurological rehabilitation therapist with extensive expertise in clinical neurology and functional rehabilitation. He is the founder of Brainstorm Rehabilitation in Port Macquarie, NSW where he develops collaborative, evidence-informed strategies to support children, adults, and families with neurological and functional health challenges.

Dr. Gray holds a Bachelor of Science from the University of Sydney (1992), a Master of Chiropractic from Macquarie University (1994), and a Master of Clinical Rehabilitation (Neurology), reflecting his advanced training in neurological assessment and rehabilitation. In 2016, he was awarded a Clinical Fellowship by the Australasian Academy of Functional Neurology in recognition of his contributions to neuroscience and functional rehabilitation.

In addition to his clinical work, Dr. Gray is a sessional lecturer in the Science and Health Departments at Charles Sturt University, Port Macquarie, New South Wales, sharing his expertise with future health professionals. His clinical approach is informed by decades of experience in sports, family health, and functional brain training, emphasizing practical, family-centered, and neuroscience-driven rehabilitation.

Vanessa Gray BEdu (HALT) DipTh

Vanessa Gray is a Highly Accomplished Teacher (HALT), one of fewer than 1% of educators in Australia to achieve this national accreditation. She holds a Bachelor of Education in Physical Development, Health and Physical Education (PDHPE) and a Graduate Certificate in Theology.

Her career began as a personal trainer, supporting clients to achieve their physical and lifestyle goals, before she moved to Japan to work as an English teacher — an experience that sparked her lifelong passion for language and cultural exchange. Over the past 25 years, she has taught across primary and secondary schools in Australia, specialising in Japanese, Physical Education, and Religious Education.

Vanessa has also held leadership roles as Sports Coordinator, curriculum developer, and mentor, supporting colleagues through evidence-based, future-focused pedagogy. Her teaching is informed by the research of John Hattie, Lyn Sharratt, Jim Knight, and Michael McDowell, with a strong focus on differentiated learning, student wellbeing, and preparing young people for an AI-driven future.

Beyond the classroom, she is a member of the Port Macquarie Hastings Council Sister City Working Group with Handa, Aichi, Japan, where she helps foster international partnerships and cultural exchange.

Her professional expertise is matched by lived experience as a parent, which grounds her work in authenticity and relatability. Together with her husband, Darren, she has lived in Port Macquarie, New South Wales since 2000, raising their two sons. The family also spends time in Japan, where they own a home and enjoy regular winter ski holidays.

INTRODUCTION: EMBRACING THE NEW WORLD OF LEARNING

OVERVIEW

Traditionally, intelligence was measured by academic achievement and career stability. However, in today's fast-evolving world, this definition no longer holds. Success is no longer assured by simply gaining entry to university. The soaring cost of higher education, coupled with rapid technological advancements, is prompting parents and students to question its value. Increasingly, graduates are leaving university burdened by debt — often disqualifying them from home loans — only to enter industries that are being disrupted or even replaced by technology and Artificial Intelligence (AI). This is the reality many graduates now face.

As parents, we all want the best for our children. We want to give them the support and opportunities we might not have had, to help them secure a future where they can thrive. We wonder, though: Will they ever be able to enter a property market that seems further out of reach with each passing year? Will they find stable, fulfilling work in a world so quickly reshaped by technology?

The future is here, and with it comes a new era of learning. Education has shifted from rote memorisation to nurturing curiosity, resilience, and adaptability. As parents, your role in this journey is more essential than ever. Rather than just helping with homework or guiding test prep, you are a partner in building the skills your child will need to navigate a world that values creativity, critical thinking, and the ability to embrace change.

In this book, we'll explore how you can support your child's growth, resilience, and curiosity, making learning an exciting and empowering part of their everyday life. The best gift we can give them isn't a formula for passing tests, but the confidence and curiosity to build a fulfilling life in a world full of new possibilities.

To truly understand the challenges and opportunities of AI in our children's lives, we need to look to the brain itself. Neuroscience reveals to us that the brain is not fixed—it is gloriously plastic, wired for growth, and constantly shaped by experience. Every moment of curiosity, every struggle with a new concept, every burst of creative play is literally sculpting new neural connections.

Artificial intelligence has the potential to become a powerful ally in education. When integrated thoughtfully, it can provide scaffolds, feedback, and opportunities that help students focus their attention and deepen their understanding. Adaptive tools can meet learners where they are, creating pathways that might otherwise remain closed.

Yet the same tools also present clear risks. Overstimulation, fragmented focus, and the temptation to bypass genuine effort can erode the very skills we hope to build. These risks remind us that technology alone cannot secure meaningful learning.

For this reason, it is essential to anchor children's digital experiences in strong neurological foundations. Healthy habits—consistent movement, restorative sleep, balanced nutrition, mindful focus, and opportunities for practice—create the conditions in which technology can truly enhance learning rather than hinder it. These habits are not optional extras; they are the bedrock of cognitive growth and resilience.

As this book unfolds, we will return to these foundations often. They provide the lens through which we can evaluate any new tool or strategy, ensuring that innovation remains grounded in what the developing brain actually needs.

In this guide, we'll explore strategies to support your child's learning journey, grounded in the latest research on how children think and grow. You'll find practical advice on creating an environment that encourages curiosity and self-motivation, along with insights on how to make mistakes part of the learning process, foster independence, and view learning as a continuous journey rather than a final product.

Today's classrooms are evolving to meet the needs of a generation with diverse strengths and limitless potential. Learning is no longer about "getting it right" on the first try; it's about exploration, asking questions, and building understanding over time. This shift encourages children to approach challenges with curiosity and resilience rather than fear of failure.

This book is here to help you navigate these changes and guide you in supporting your child's unique learning journey, making education an exciting and enriching part of family life. With the insights and strategies shared in these pages, you'll be able to foster a love for discovery, both in your child and within yourself. Together, we can adopt this new approach, cultivating lifelong learners who are ready to thrive in a world filled with opportunities and challenges.

The Learning Brain: Unlocking the Neuroscience of Education

Neuroplasticity is the brain's remarkable ability to reorganise itself by forming new neural connections throughout life. Think of your brain as a vast network of pathways - much like roads connecting different suburbs. When you learn something new, your brain literally rewrites these pathways, creating stronger connections between neurons and even growing new ones.

This discovery revolutionised our understanding of learning. Previously, scientists believed the adult brain was fixed and unchangeable. We now know that "your brain changes physically whenever you learn anything, and your brain continues to be moulded by experience and learning throughout your life." The neurons that "fire together, wire together," strengthening the pathways you use most frequently.

Recent brain research has moved well beyond Carol Dweck's important work by directly linking growth mindset with neuroplasticity - the brain's ability to physically rewire itself. Contemporary studies demonstrate that teaching students about their brain's capacity for change creates measurable improvements in motivation and academic achievement. This works because neuroplasticity means our neural connections literally strengthen when we learn, with research showing that memories are encoded by physical changes in the brain (UNESCO, 2021).

Brain imaging reveals that children who believe they can improve actually process mistakes differently, seeing them as learning opportunities rather than failures. Modern neuroplasticity research confirms that the brain continues changing throughout life, supporting learning and memory formation (Pascoe et al., 2025). Today's educational neuroscience combines brain science with emotional and social learning because neuroplasticity responds to both intellectual challenge and emotional engagement (Karpouzian et al., 2022).

The significance is clear: when students understand their brains physically change through effort, they create the very neural rewiring that makes learning possible. This represents a fundamental shift from viewing intelligence as fixed to understanding it as developable through the brain's remarkable plasticity.

This has profound implications for teaching and learning.

Neuroplasticity "encompasses a range of mechanisms, including changes in synaptic strength and connectivity, the formation of new synapses, alterations in the structure and function of neurons, and the generation of new neurons." It means that struggle and mistakes aren't signs of failure - they're essential parts of the brain-building process.

Understanding neuroplasticity empowers both educators and learners, proving that intelligence isn't fixed - with effort and appropriate strategies, anyone can strengthen their cognitive abilities throughout their lifetime.

Neuroplasticity revolutionises education by proving intelligence isn't fixed. Research shows that understanding the brain's ability to rewire itself through effort dramatically improves student performance. This knowledge transforms teaching approaches, empowering educators and learners to embrace challenges as brain-building opportunities, fundamentally changing how we approach lifelong learning and human potential.

PART ONE:
OVERWHELMED

CHAPTER 1:
THE TRUTH ABOUT MODERN LEARNING

We are raising children in a time unlike any other. My own children aren't rushing to use AI—they're reluctant. Not because they don't understand it, but because they're unsure what's allowed and the impact on their careers. My eldest recently told me, "Mum, every time you use AI, you're taking away jobs from my generation." That hit hard. It's a sentiment echoed by many of my colleagues, whispered behind classroom doors and spoken aloud in staff meetings: Will we be replaced? I see it differently. I believe we're just getting started.

The rules have changed—and in many ways, so has the game. In many ways this moment feels like the 1950s race to put a man on the moon, a global acceleration where nations, industries and school systems are moving faster to understand, build, and harness a technology that will reshape the future. The countries that moved early in the space race shaped the next half of the century. The same will be true now with AI. We're standing in a once in a lifetime shift and the decisions we make for our children today will echo into their opportunities tomorrow. Today's students don't just learn with textbooks. They learn through YouTube tutorials, Discord conversations, TikTok explainers, Roblox builds, and AI-powered platforms like Perplexity, ChatGPT, Copilot, and Gemini. Their learning is nonlinear, multi-modal, and often self-initiated. In many cases, they're experimenting with these tools before their teachers — or parents — fully understand what they are.

And yet, even digital natives feel the weight of uncertainty. They're not leaping blindly into this future; they're hesitating at the edge. They know these tools are powerful, but they don't yet know how to use them ethically. They crave guidance — not rigid rules, but wisdom, reflection, and safety.

That's where we come in.

As both a teacher and a parent, I don't see AI as the end of learning. I see it as a mirror: one that reflects who we are, what we value, and where we're heading. It challenges us to rethink not just what we teach—but why, how, and for whom. It urges us to reconsider how we measure growth, motivate students, and connect across the digital divide.

When people say teachers will be replaced by AI, I ask: Did we learn nothing during COVID lockdowns? The world couldn't wait to bring children back into classrooms—not just for academic instruction, but for connection. For community. For care.

I had never felt so overworked and underappreciated as I did in that season. While teachers scrambled to reinvent learning overnight, many in the community spoke as though the "real work" only resumed when children returned to classrooms and parents could return to their jobs. It was exhausting and, at times, disheartening. Yet beneath the pressure, one truth became undeniable:

students weren't just missing worksheets and lessons. They were aching for the laughter in corridors, the eye contact of peers, the unspoken safety of belonging.

If it were as simple as a teacher being replaced by a chatbot, then maybe we need to reflect on what kind of teaching is taking place.

Because real teaching has never been about content delivery. It's about building humans—holding space for their questions, shaping their resilience, and reminding them that they are more than a grade on a screen.

And what makes us human is not just our intelligence, but our emotional depth—our empathy, resilience, perspective-taking, and capacity for connection. These skills—often grouped under emotional intelligence—are not just nice-to-haves; they are essential. They are what differentiate students in a world where AI can already pass medical exams and write legal briefs.

Socratic Thinking in the AI Era

Socratic thinking is the disciplined practice of asking and answering questions to deepen understanding, challenge assumptions, and uncover meaning. Named after the philosopher Socrates, it places inquiry above memorisation and dialogue above passive reception. In a world where artificial intelligence can generate instant answers, this approach must become the new way of learning.

John Hattie's landmark research in Visible Learning consistently shows that questioning, feedback, and classroom dialogue are among the most powerful influences on student achievement. Socratic thinking embodies these practices, training children not just to absorb information but to interrogate it, weigh it, and extend it. The skill that will set them apart in the AI era is not the knowledge they recall, but the quality of the questions they learn to ask.

This shift doesn't only belong in classrooms — it starts at home. Imagine your child asks an AI LLM (Large

Language Model) to summarise a science concept. Instead of saying "Great, you've got the answer," you could lean in with questions such as, "What's missing from that explanation?", "Do you agree with it? Why or why not?", or "How could you explain this to your younger sibling?" These small but deliberate prompts turn AI from an answer machine into a thinking partner. They also model for your child that your interest isn't in the product alone, but in their process of reasoning and reflection.

We must prepare children not to compete with AI, but to complement it. To bring what machines cannot: emotional nuance, ethical reasoning, creative empathy, and human insight.

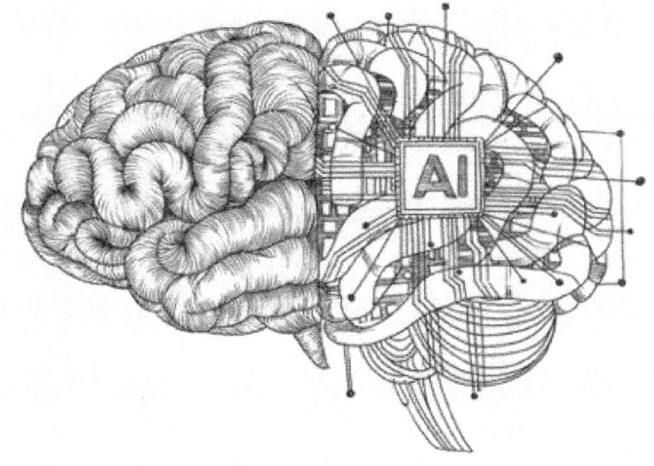

Artificial Intelligence isn't replacing humans. Artificial Intelligence is amplifying humans. The future belongs to children who can partner with intelligent tools while staying deeply, unmistakably human.

Meanwhile, in countries like China, children as young as six are being introduced to AI through coding toys, adaptive robots, and structured programs that weave machine learning into maths and language curricula. Leaders such as Derek Haoyang Li, founder of Squirrel AI, are already scaling adaptive learning platforms across thousands of schools, while researchers like

Xiangen Hu are shaping intelligent tutoring systems grounded in the science of how children learn. Thinkers such as Kai-Fu Lee, in AI Superpowers and AI 2041, highlights that these initiatives are not isolated — they reflect China's national commitment, led by the Ministry of Education, to embed AI literacy from the ground up. These children aren't just learning to use AI; they are being taught to think algorithmically, to problem-solve alongside machines, and to understand AI's place in the world.

If we don't help our own children engage with these tools — and with themselves — we risk falling behind not only technologically, but emotionally, ethically, and socially.

Digital Learning and the Brain: Ben's Transformation

Darren points out that when we talk about learning differences, we're not talking about choices children make. We're talking about how their brains are wired. He puts it like this:

"ADHD isn't a behaviour problem. It's a regulation problem in the brain's executive function system — the prefrontal cortex. That's where attention, impulse control, and working memory live. In kids with ADHD, a chemical signal- neurotransmitter, like dopamine isn't released in the right amounts at the right times. That's why sitting still in a conventional classroom feels like torture: their brain isn't being fuelled by the reward pathways it needs to stay engaged."

Ben was one of those kids in Year 6 — sharp as a tack, but always on the move. He'd fidget in his chair, eyes darting from the whiteboard to the window to whatever was inside his pencil case. The usual classroom strategies just didn't cut it. His parents and teachers tried everything: different seating, quick brain breaks, visual tools, even extra one-on-one time. Each made a small difference, but none really solved the gap between how Ben's brain worked and what the classroom expected.

The turning point came with a digital cognitive training platform built to work with the ADHD brain, rather than against it.

Darren explains why this brain based therapy approached made such a difference:

Ben had always struggled to stay engaged — his brain's attention systems would tire quickly with traditional methods. The application of a digital learning platform changed that by working with how his brain naturally learns. Instant feedback released feel-good chemicals that helped reinforce his focus. Using multiple senses — sight, sound, and movement — activated different brain areas at the same time, strengthening the connections between brain cells. "Neurons that fire together, wire together" is the basic principle of how our brains learn and adapt through practice.

The digital AI therapy system kept the difficulty at just the right level — challenging enough to promote growth but not so hard as to cause stress. Game-like rewards tapped into the brain's natural motivation system, keeping him engaged. Instead of working against how his brain functioned, the platform worked with it — allowing real, lasting changes in brain structure to develop.

The results spoke for themselves. Within just a few weeks, Ben was able to sustain his concentration throughout the school day — a shift in his cognitive fitness that had once seemed impossible. His literacy and numeracy also began to improve, not because the platform directly "taught" him new content, but because his brain was finally able to stay with the material long enough to process it.

Most powerful of all was the change in his self-image: he no longer saw himself as "the distracted kid," but as a student who was capable, focused, and ready to learn. Ben's story is proof of something bigger.

As Darren explains,

"When we design learning to match how the brain actually works, we don't just improve performance; we restore a child's

belief in themselves. And that belief is what rewires everything."

The Challenge for Parents

For many parents, the pace of change feels dizzying. One moment you're helping with a long division. Next, you're being asked to check a citation in an AI-generated summary. It's disorienting.

You might feel unsure, even excluded. You may worry that your child is sprinting ahead in a digital world you weren't raised in. But I want to tell you this: your role has never been more vital.

Your child doesn't need you to be a tech expert. They need you to be a wise, curious guide. They need someone who asks thoughtful questions, who models lifelong learning, and who holds the line on values, safety, and emotional regulation. They need you to talk about what's ethical, what's real, what matters. AI can't do that. But you can.

Let your home be a place of open dialogue and shared discovery. Explore tools together. Discuss what's helpful, what's harmful, and what's possible. Let your child know that they're not navigating this alone.

Most importantly, support their emotional development in parallel with their digital fluency. Help them name their feelings, regulate their frustrations, and develop self-awareness as they move through increasingly complex digital and social spaces. Because in the age of AI, emotional intelligence isn't just an asset — it's a survival skill.

Guardrails and Guidelines: A Call to Schools

This shift doesn't stop at home. Schools must evolve, too. Literacy now means more than decoding text — it must include digital fluency, prompt design, critical reading of AI outputs, and ethical engagement with tools. Prompt engineering isn't a novelty — it's the new handwriting.

We must rethink how we teach writing, research, creativity, and originality. Assessment should measure thinking, not regurgitation. Feedback should support reflection, not just correction. None of this happens by accident. It takes leadership, clear policy, and courageous conversations.

Let's raise children who don't just use AI—but who question it, co-create with it, and challenge its assumptions. Because the future isn't something we prepare children for. It's something we prepare them to shape.

And in Chapter 13, we'll go even deeper—exploring how these guardrails become lifelines for children whose brains are wired differently, and how AI can either widen or close the gap for those learners depending on the choices we make today.

Parent Reflection Prompts

- When was the last time I felt uncertain about the tools my child is using to learn?
- What assumptions do I hold about screen time—and are they still serving our family?
- Have my conversations about technology come from a place of fear—or possibility?

- How do I model curiosity, critical thinking, and lifelong learning at home?
- How am I helping my child develop emotional intelligence, not just digital competence?
- What values do I want to pass on as we navigate this AI-powered world together?

The future isn't something we prepare children for — it's something we prepare them to shape.

Let's walk beside them — not behind.

CHAPTER 2:
GAMER MINDS – TURNING PLAY INTO PURPOSE

Understanding AI and Gaming in Your Child's Education

As a parent, you might wonder how technology is reshaping your child's learning experience. AI and gaming are increasingly working together in educational settings, creating exciting new ways for children to learn.

Think of AI as a smart tutor that adapts to your child's individual learning pace. When combined with educational games, it can adjust difficulty levels in real-time, ensuring your child isn't overwhelmed or bored. For instance, if your child struggles with maths, an AI-powered educational game might offer extra practice problems or present concepts differently until they grasp the material.

Gaming in education isn't about entertainment alone — it's about engagement. Educational games capture children's natural curiosity and motivation, making learning feel less like work and more like play. Meanwhile, AI ensures the experience remains educational by tracking progress, identifying knowledge gaps, and providing personalised feedback.

We need to shift the philosophy of education when preparing students for an AI-driven workforce — from creating generators to creating evaluators. In a world where large language models and image tools can produce endless streams of content, our children will need the ability to navigate deep fakes, assess accuracy, and distinguish between AI-generated and human-generated work. This shift isn't just about academic integrity; it's about equipping them with the capacity to question, verify, and judge credibility in a landscape where truth is increasingly blurred.

This combination helps develop critical thinking, problem-solving skills, and digital literacy — essential capabilities for your child's future. Rather than replacing traditional teaching, these technologies complement classroom learning, offering interactive experiences that make abstract concepts tangible and memorable for young minds. When AI is used alongside skilled teachers, it doesn't diminish learning; it enhances it, providing new pathways for curiosity, creativity, and discernment. The goal is not to raise children who can out-generate the machines, but ones who can evaluate, interpret, and apply what those machines produce with wisdom and integrity.

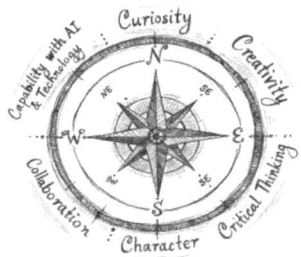

Kai sat at the back of my Year 7 Japanese class, head down, doing just enough to get by. He wasn't disruptive—just distant. He'd already made it clear he had no plans to study Japanese beyond the compulsory year. Written tasks were rushed, oral activities mumbled.

But one day, I introduced a simple AI tool that translated his English phrases into Japanese and read them aloud. I told him he didn't need to produce perfect sentences—just pick something he wanted to say and try repeating what the AI said.

Something shifted. Kai listened carefully, then started mimicking the pronunciation. At first, it was just one word. Then a phrase. Then a full sentence. He wasn't suddenly fluent—but he was engaged.It turned out, Kai didn't dislike Japanese. He just didn't believe he could say anything right. The AI gave him a model, and that model gave him confidence. For the first time, he could hear himself getting better—and that changed everything about how he showed up in class.

This is what I see in classrooms every day: a generation of learners wired for interaction, challenge, and story.

They navigate virtual and physical spaces fluidly, often outpacing adults in adapting to new platforms. And while many adults worry that games are a distraction or even a danger, I see something different—a profound opportunity to harness the very habits that make gaming so compelling, and turn them into purposeful learning.

The Neurological Benefits of Gaming

As parents, we naturally want to support our children's learning and development. One emerging tool that's showing remarkable promise is AI-powered gaming – and the science behind its benefits is fascinating.

Think of your child's brain as a bustling construction site. Every day, millions of neural connections are being built,

strengthened, or pruned away. This incredible adaptability, called neuroplasticity, means your child's brain is constantly reshaping itself based on experiences. AI games create rich, adaptive environments that take advantage of this natural flexibility, allowing children to exercise various cognitive functions while promoting healthy brain plasticity.

You might wonder: does screen time actually help my child's thinking skills? The research is encouraging. Studies show that children who engage with well-designed games demonstrate faster and more accurate performance on cognitive tasks, with measurable positive changes in brain function. Unlike passive screen time, AI gaming actively challenges your child's mind, creating an environment where learning and entertainment merge seamlessly.

Perhaps most importantly, AI gaming strengthens what neuroscientists call executive functions – your child's mental toolkit for success. These games help develop the critical abilities that enable children to think before acting, solve unexpected problems, resist distractions, and maintain concentration. Research consistently shows improvements in both sustained attention and selective attention, with corresponding positive changes in the brain regions responsible for attention control. These skills extend far beyond gaming, supporting academic performance and social interactions.

The key is achieving neurological balance—moderate gaming with educational content.

Reframing the Fears

Many parents fear that gaming is replacing real life—that it disconnects children from the world around them, fuels addiction, or nurtures aggression. These fears aren't unfounded. Left unchecked, digital play can overstimulate the brain's reward circuits and make everyday tasks feel dull by comparison.

But not all screen time is equal. Educational psychologist Jane Healy (2020) encourages parents to distinguish between active and passive screen time. Watching YouTube passively for three hours is not the same as solving logic puzzles in a coding platform or designing a biome in Minecraft.

Darren elaborates:

"When a child is deeply focused on a challenge – adjusting variables, experimenting, failing, and retrying – we see activation in the prefrontal cortex, which governs critical thinking. These are the same regions engaged during inquiry-based learning."

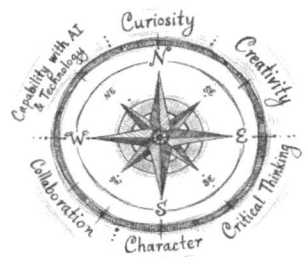

Real Classrooms, Real Growth

In my Year 8 Japanese class, I introduced a gamified vocabulary competition using Quizizz Live. Two things happened:

- Students who had previously been disengaged — especially boys who struggled with rote memorisation — suddenly came alive.
- One neurodivergent student, often overwhelmed by social interaction, volunteered to lead his team's strategy.

What changed? The game offered immediate feedback, clear goals, peer validation, and low-risk failure. For that student, AI-generated prompts in Japanese allowed him to rehearse phrases silently before speaking, reducing anxiety and increasing confidence.

Another example: a Year 7 class full of diverse learners — some with ADHD, others with trauma backgrounds, some academically gifted, others deeply disengaged. Traditional instruction failed. So I created a role-play activity: students became "language agents" decoding Japanese messages using Gemini as a dictionary, and kanji puzzles. Even my most disruptive student asked to stay in at lunch to "finish the mission."

These transformations didn't happen because of the tech alone. They happened because I used tech with relational trust, emotional scaffolding, and intentional design.

Gaming and Neurodivergence

Neurodivergence describes natural variations in neurological development and brain function, encompassing conditions such as ADHD, autism spectrum disorders, dyslexia, dyspraxia, and Tourette syndrome. These differences arise from variations in neural circuitry —

particularly in regions that govern executive function, attention regulation, sensory processing, social cognition, and language. From a neuroscientific perspective, neurodivergent brains show distinct patterns in neurotransmitter systems such as dopamine and serotonin, altered cortical connectivity, and unique activation in areas like the prefrontal cortex, temporal lobes, and cerebellum. The result is not deficit, but diversity: distinct learning profiles, sensory sensitivities, and cognitive processing styles.

Understanding neurodivergence in education means recognising that children's brains are wired to process information through different pathways. Inclusive frameworks affirm this diversity, using multimodal teaching, sensory-

aware environments, and individualised support to work with, rather than against, a child's natural wiring.

Digital tools and gaming offer both opportunities and risks in this context. For students with ADHD, the short feedback loops and built-in reward systems of games provide the rapid dopamine hits their brains crave, helping sustain attention. For anxious learners, predictable game structures create safety and control. For children on the autism spectrum, games provide a rule-governed rehearsal ground for turn-taking and social interaction. As Darren often puts it, "Think of your child's brain like a road map. Every new experience lays down a path, and the more often it's travelled, the smoother and faster it becomes. Digital activities don't just fill time—they reinforce certain routes over and over, shaping which roads become highways, just like practice makes a skill second nature."

Well-designed digital experiences can strengthen problem-solving, cognitive flexibility, and resilience by engaging the brain's executive functions. Dopamine release in response to small wins promotes persistence and motivation. Yet without balance, the same reward systems can drive impulsivity or over-reliance on external validation, leaving children struggling with slower, less stimulating real-world activities.

The key is intentional use: quality digital experiences combined with varied offline activities, appropriate challenge, and co-engagement with parents. This neurodiversity-affirming approach not only optimises brain development, but also empowers children to build confidence and resilience by working with the way their brains naturally learn.

Family Story: When Gaming Sparked an Argument

Parenting together doesn't always mean parenting in sync.

One evening, our older son was deep in a gaming mission—headphones on, eyes locked, completely absorbed. Hours had slipped by when Vanessa walked into the lounge. Her voice was firm, no room for negotiation

"Enough. Switch it off now." I could see his whole body stiffen. He was mid-mission, adrenaline high, his prefrontal cortex still locked into the game. Pulling him out at that moment was like slamming the brakes on a car at full speed. Frustration was inevitable.

"Let him finish this round, Ness," I said gently. "Cutting him off now will only end in a blow-up."

But Vanessa wasn't thinking about brain states. She was thinking about boundaries — about the risk of screens taking over. We clashed: I argued from the science, she stood firm in her instinct, and our son sat silently between us

Later that night, once things had cooled, we admitted the truth. We were both scared. Scared that gaming would swallow too much of our son's time. Scared that our different approaches would confuse him.

Out of that tension, we worked out a new rhythm. Our son could finish the level — but only if he gave us a clear estimate of the time left. In return, he agreed to stick to our boundaries without sneaking in "just one more round."

That night mattered. Not because we found the perfect solution, but because he saw us wrestle with it honestly. He saw that even adults argue, reflect, and then compromise. And maybe that was the most important lesson of all.

Parent as Co-Pilot

To harness the benefits of gaming, parents don't need to become gamers. But they do need to be curious, open, and engaged. Try sitting beside your child for 10 minutes during a game session. Ask:

- "What's the goal in this game?"
- "What was your biggest challenge today?"
- "What strategy did you change mid-game?"
- "If you were the designer, how would you improve this level?"

These questions invite reflection. They turn play into metacognition. They show your child that you're not there to control their screen time—but to understand their world.

Practical Ways Parents Can Harness the Gamer Mindset

- **Turn Real-Life Tasks into Quests**
  Design a week-long mission where your child tackles a real-world challenge—planning a family dinner, creating a budget, designing a pet enclosure. Break it into levels. Offer power-ups (small rewards). Use AI tools like Perplexity to support their research.
- **Create a Screen Time Agreement Together**
  Include:
  – Minimum outdoor time
  – Homework and chores before play
  – Clear game types (educational vs social vs solo)
  When children help design the rules, they're more likely to respect them.

- **Try Educational Platforms That Feel Like Games**

    Explore tools like Scratch (coding), Prodigy (maths), or Duolingo (languages) together. Celebrate effort, not just progress.

- **Apply Gaming Logic to Study Habits**

    Encourage strategies like:

    – Breaking tasks into "levels"

    – Earning small rewards after focus sessions

    – Tracking progress visually

These approaches mirror game dynamics and make learning feel achievable.

A Bigger Picture

Gaming isn't just an activity — it is a form of literacy. Today's students learn through systems, storylines, feedback loops, and social negotiation. These are 21st-century learning skills. Our role isn't to fight it. It's to frame it. To help children use what they love to develop who they're becoming.

What if your child's screen obsession isn't a problem to solve—but a pathway to understand how they think, what motivates them, and how they cope with challenges?

Gaming isn't the enemy of education. It's a powerful ally when used with guidance. In this new world, our job isn't to fear the tools; it's to harness them. It's to co-pilot them. Because when play meets purpose, and curiosity meets challenge, our children don't just learn. They thrive. They level up for life.

Parent Reflection Prompts

- What does gaming offer my child that other activities might not?
- Have I explored their favourite games with curiosity, or only critique?
- How can I support them to apply their in-game problem-solving to real-world tasks?
- What values do I want to reinforce through the way I respond to their digital lives?

Final Thought

Gaming isn't merely about screens, scores, or survival modes. At its core, it is a powerful environment where young minds are actively learning to tackle challenges, adapt strategies, and persist through failure. In clinical and educational contexts, we understand that these are the very skills associated with resilience and executive functioning. Yes, gaming can cause conflict at home — as Darren and I have both observed. But it can also serve as a bridge: a unique lens into how children think, what motivates them, and how they interpret their world.

When parents shift from the role of gatekeepers — focused only on restriction — to that of co-pilots, something important changes. Gaming ceases to be a battleground and becomes a dynamic classroom. Not the classroom of chalkboards and rows of desks, but one defined by creativity, strategic problem-solving, and persistence in the face of setbacks. This is where lessons in emotional regulation, teamwork, and adaptive thinking are rehearsed and reinforced in real time.

The real question for parents isn't "How do I make my child stop gaming?" It is, 'How do I help my child find the connection between their online skills and their real life potential?", because the skills they're building behind the screen - strategy, collaboration, creativity, persistence are the very same strengths that can help them thrive beyond their gaming world.

CHAPTER 3:
RETHINKING SUCCESS – SKILLS FOR A CHANGING WORLD

In my early teaching years, "success" was a word wrapped in ATAR (Australian Tertiary Admissions Rank) scores, exam rankings, and university acceptance letters. But these days, I find myself asking more profound questions: Is that success? Is it enough? In a world where AI can already write code, compose music, and draft essays, our children's future won't be built on regurgitating knowledge—but on creativity, empathy, and adaptability.

One student, Layla, reminded me of this. She didn't excel in tests, but could take a group of tense, off-task students and turn them into a cohesive team. During a project-based Religion unit, she organised her group's timeline, allocated tasks fairly, and coached peers through conflict resolution. The result wasn't just a polished final product—it was a lesson in leadership. Layla may never be Dux, but she's already more "future-ready" than most.

What Does Success Mean Now?

The World Economic Forum (2023) identifies problem-solving, self-management, resilience, and technology use as the top skills required for 21st-century learners. Similarly, education researcher Yong Zhao argues that "in an age of smart machines, human uniqueness becomes the new currency."

As a teacher and a parent, this resonates deeply. We need to broaden our definition of achievement.

Success must include:

- The ability to collaborate across cultures and contexts
- Emotional intelligence and mental wellbeing
- Curiosity-driven learning
- Comfort with failure and ambiguity

Darren points out, "Brains that are rewarded only for compliance and accuracy become risk-averse. But brains rewarded for exploration, reflection, and connection build richer neural networks—networks better suited for long-term growth in a rapidly shifting world."

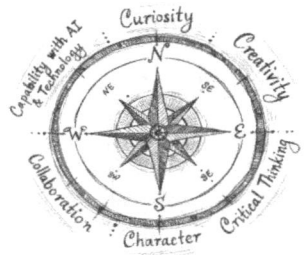

From the Front Lines: A Tale of Two Learners

In a Year 8 Japanese class, I had two students: Tyler and Nathan. Tyler was the model student—always punctual, neat, and diligent. He followed instructions to the letter, often producing textbook-perfect work. Nathan, on the other hand, was often distracted, frequently sketching in the margins of his book or talking about new tech tools he was experimenting with at home.

For an assessment task, students were asked to create a travel presentation about Japan. Most students—including Tyler—used Google Slides to highlight a few major cities, inserted neatly formatted text and basic images, and presented a standard itinerary. It was good, but safe. Tyler's work earned him a high mark—he had followed every instruction.

Nathan approached the task differently.

He used AI tools like Gemini and CoPilot to dive deeper into Japanese geography, festivals, and subcultures. Then, instead of making a traditional slideshow, he created a clickable interactive map of Japan, where each destination unlocked a digital "experience." Users could click on Kyoto to take a virtual temple tour, Tokyo to simulate navigating a train station with Japanese phrases, or Hokkaido to explore regional foods via an AI-generated menu. He embedded visuals, cultural facts, audio clips, and even a short AI-written travel conversation in Japanese.

It was captivating. And completely outside the box.

Tyler ticked every requirement on the rubric. Nathan reimagined the task entirely. Both received good marks, but only one of them showed the kind of innovation, initiative, and digital storytelling that reflects the real skills our students need today.

This experience echoes the work of Robert J. Sternberg, a renowned psychologist and education researcher, who argues that traditional assessment measures only a narrow slice of student potential. Standardised tasks and rigid rubrics often reward what Sternberg calls analytical intelligence, but overlook the importance of creativity, ethical reasoning, and practical application—what he terms successful intelligence.

As Sternberg notes:

"These tests do account for analytical skills, but they do not assess creative skills, practical skills, or wisdom-based ethical skills."

And more provocatively:

"My beef ... is that the tests don't find the people who are going to change the world."

This could have been said about Nathan. Nathan didn't just complete the task—he transformed it. In doing so, he revealed abilities that no standard test could measure. And in a world where students must increasingly combine language, culture, and digital fluency, that kind of risk-taking matters far more than polished compliance.

Traditional schooling often rewards those who master the system. But the future will belong to those who design the system, question it, and imagine something better. As educators and parents, we need to recognise and nurture those abilities—not just reward the tidy, compliant ones.

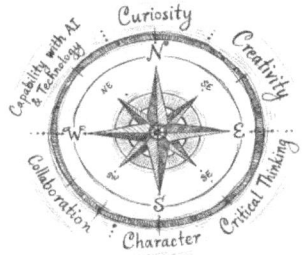

Japanese Class Snapshot: When Curiosity Wins

In a Year 7 Japanese lesson, we were exploring the difference between formal and casual greetings. Most students dutifully copied notes. But Emily, a quieter student with ASD, became fascinated by the context of formality in Japanese society. She independently asked our classroom AI assistant, Gemini, "Why do Japanese people bow instead of shake hands?"

Gemini responded with a cultural insight that sparked a five-minute class discussion—something Emily usually avoided. That moment didn't just teach Japanese etiquette—it nurtured confidence, inquiry, and a genuine interest in intercultural understanding.

Redefining the Metrics: From Grades to Growth

Psychologist Carol Dweck's research on growth mindset shows us that intelligence isn't fixed—it's cultivated. When we celebrate effort, strategy, and progress over performance, we don't just build achievers—we build resilient learners who persist through failure and adapt to challenges.

In the context of a rapidly globalising world, this mindset shift becomes even more crucial. While students of the future may not need to speak a foreign language fluently — thanks to real-time translation tools and AI — they will need to understand how to operate respectfully within another culture. Cultural sensitivity, global competence, and the ability to navigate nuance across borders will become defining traits of future-ready learners.

As Dr Darren Gray explains

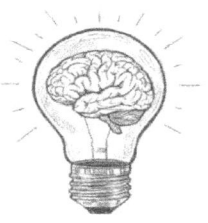

"Your child's brain is a powerful learning system, constantly rewiring through neuroplasticity. Since the prefrontal cortex — the brain's "CEO" — doesn't fully mature until around age 25, childhood and adolescence are prime years to strengthen these networks. Mistakes aren't

setbacks; they're fuel for growth. Each struggle activates neurotransmitters like dopamine and norepinephrine, while the brain refines strategies and builds stronger pathways.

In an AI-driven world, this process becomes even more valuable. AI isn't a replacement for thinking — it's a partner in it. When guided well, children learn to use AI to ask sharper questions, test ideas, and expand understanding. These "desirable difficulties" build resilience, metacognition, and the critical thinking skills they'll need for life."training the brain to be flexible, empathetic, and culturally aware.

AI Is Redefining the Future of Work — not Replacing It

Artificial Intelligence is already reshaping workplaces across industries — from healthcare systems using it for early diagnostics to retail giants leveraging it for inventory forecasting. The pivotal question isn't whether AI will take jobs; it's how jobs will evolve — and how our children can thrive in a world shaped by it.

According to the Future of Jobs Report 2025 from the World Economic Forum (WEF) AI will displace around 92 million roles by 2030 — but it will also create an estimated 170 million new, often higher-paying jobs. That's a net increase of 78 million opportunities for adaptable, proactive individuals.

This shift places a premium not just on technical expertise but on distinctly human strengths. A recent WEF study underscores that soft skills — such as communication, ethics, and teamwork — are rising in value precisely because AI is widening their gap with machines.

Policy-focused organisations like the Organisation for Economic Co-operation and OECD echo this. Their 'AI and the Future of Skills' project highlights the importance of aligning education and training with the evolving landscape, ensuring humans remain complementary — not competitive — to AI.

As noted in the New Skills Triad from WEF's 2023 report, the ability to combine AI fluency, 'virtual intelligence' (the savvy interaction with machine outputs), and ethical thinking is fast becoming the foundational blueprint for future careers.

Upskilling will not be an option — it will be a necessity. As one business leader warned, "Lifelong learning will become the most crucial skill for future job market relevance." We've already seen new AI-focused programs launching in universities globally, from master's degrees to micro-credentials — all blending technical literacy with ethical reasoning and creativity.

So, what does this mean for parents — and for students?

It's not about fearing the robot — or burying heads in the sand. It's about steering toward optimism: raising children who know how to use AI as a creative tool, a partner, not a crutch. It's about nurturing the flexible, curious, empathetic, and resilient learners who will shape a future we can't yet fully imagine. So how can we shift our home environments to align with this?

Practical Tips for Parents: Supporting Real-World Readiness

1. Praise the Process, Not the Product

Instead of "You're so smart," try: "You stuck with that even when it was hard." It rewires the reward system to value perseverance.

2. Invite Your Child to Teach You Something

Whether it's showing you how to use ChatGPT or Gemini or explaining a YouTuber's editing style, teaching activates deeper understanding—and signals that their interests are valid.

3. Explore Diverse Definitions of Success

Watch a documentary about an Olympic athlete who didn't win gold. Read a story about a social entrepreneur. Celebrate the risk-takers, the creatives, the quiet contributors.

4. Use AI to Support — Not Replace — Learning

Ask tools like Gemini or Copilot to suggest steps for a research project, but encourage your child to personalise, evaluate, and reflect. Critical engagement matters more than speed.

5. Expose Them to Passion-Based Pathways

From esports commentary to ethical hacking, the job landscape is changing. Let them explore what lights them up — even if it doesn't look like a "real" job yet.

6. Reinforce Non-Academic Strengths

Create a "life skills board" at home and include moments like calming a sibling, organising a schedule, or researching how to fix a bike chain. These are real achievements.

7. Take an AI Walkabout

Pick a topic and ask your child to compare answers across two AI platforms — e.g. Perplexity vs Gemini vs ChatGPT. Discuss differences. This builds digital discernment and invites conversation.

My Son, the Square Peg

Our eldest son was bright, compassionate, and talented — but school never quite fit. He dragged himself through to the end of Year 11, but only just. For months, we were walking on egg shells around him. We changed his schools, adjusted expectations, tried everything we could think of to make things easier, yet nothing seemed to reach him. We told ourselves he was just tired, unmotivated, maybe going through a phase. What we couldn't see, what was right there in front of us was his quiet, consuming depression. One morning, when he hadn't arrived at school I rang him. He said that he was sitting in his car crying. He said 'Mum I do this everyday'. He wasn't staying at school because he believed in the path ahead — he was staying because he thought it was what we wanted. His psychologist gently confirmed what I already feared: he was enduring school for our sake.

The revelation hit like a physical blow — my beautiful son, sitting alone in his car each morning, tears streaming down his face before forcing himself through another day of academic torture. He was emotionally and physically sapped! At that moment, I saw the cruel irony clearly. We'd been so determined to help him "succeed" that we'd ignored his quiet desperation and cries for help.

His light was fading, sacrificed to a system that measured worth in ways that didn't recognise his gifts. The bright, compassionate child who once approached the world with wonder had learned to see himself as failing, simply because traditional schooling couldn't accommodate the way he wanted to move forward. We'd inadvertently taught him that our approval mattered more than his wellbeing.

Importantly, we realised sometimes love means letting go of the path we imagined and trusting our children to find their own way forward. Real success isn't about fitting in — it's about flourishing authentically.

Parent Reflection Prompts

- What strengths does my child show outside of academics?

- Have I praised their process—or only their outcomes?
- What new forms of success could we explore together this month?
- Which "real-world" skill or strength has gone unnoticed until now?
- Have I unknowingly sent the message that their passion isn't valid?
- What does "thriving" look like for my child—not just someone else's?

Final Thought

Let's redefine success—not as a scorecard, but as a mindset where curiosity, collaboration, and character matter as much as content. When we do, we empower our children not merely to survive the future, but to shape it. In the end, the most valuable measure may not be what they know, but who they are becoming. Success in the age of AI will hinge on how well our children regulate themselves, recover from setbacks, and connect meaningfully with others. Their brains need novelty, but also reflection. They crave both challenge and belonging. When we nurture that balance, we raise not just achievers—but thinkers, feelers, and leaders.

PART TWO: UNDERSTOOD

CHAPTER 4:
BUILDING A GROWTH MINDSET IN AN AI WORLD

Mia slumped in her chair, staring at the worksheet in front of her. "I'm just not good at this," she muttered. Her teacher knelt beside her and asked gently, "What if you just haven't figured it out—yet?" That one word—yet—planted a seed. It suggested a possibility, a future where effort mattered more than talent. And that changed everything.

In our classrooms, that shift—from fixed to growth mindset—can be the turning point not just for learning outcomes, but for wellbeing, resilience, and the capacity to thrive in a changing world. In a culture where AI can instantly generate essays, correct spelling, or answer factual questions, the difference between learners won't be who knows more—but who keeps trying when things get hard.

The Science of 'Yet'

Psychologist Carol Dweck coined the term "growth mindset" to describe the belief that abilities can be developed through dedication and effort. Here's where Darren's perspective is valuable. "Every time a child tackles a challenge and gets feedback—whether they succeed or stumble—their brain is busy strengthening pathways in the prefrontal cortex. That part of the brain is like the control centre for planning, self-regulation, and creativity. The more those pathways are reinforced, the stronger these lifelong skills become." Repeated effort isn't just character-building—it's brain-building.

When students believe mistakes are signs of progress, they become more likely to engage in learning and less likely to give up. AI can amplify this by offering adaptive feedback, which provides suggestions without judgment, allowing students to edit, reframe, and retry in real-time.

However, and this is crucial, it's the mindset, not the tool, that fosters lasting change. AI is a mirror. If a child sees feedback as a threat, they'll close off. If they see it as a map, they'll take the next step.

The Nerve That Changed Everything

What began as routine varicose vein surgery became the greatest test of our lives.

I walked into the hospital room still wearing my shirt and tie from an online interview for a university lecturer position in Malaysia; buzzing with possibility. But the moment I saw Vanessa, everything else faded. She looked unsettled — her leg was completely numb.

We reassured ourselves it was just the anaesthetic nerve block. The ward nurse and family members reassured us and suggested we do the same. But when the anaesthetist checked the next morning and she still couldn't feel anything, my stomach dropped.

The days that followed felt endless. Nerve conduction studies and MRIs crawled by at the pace that regional

New South Wales healthcare allows. When the results came back, the verdict was devastating: minimal nerve conduction. The surgeon had likely severed her common peroneal nerve during the procedure. Permanent damage. Foot drop. No more running, no more teaching PE, possibly no walking without pain.

But something didn't sit right with me. I'd just completed my clinical neurology degree, and every instinct I'd developed said this wasn't right. The nerve wasn't severed—compressed perhaps, inflamed maybe, but not cut. I told Vanessa I believed her nerve was still intact.

When she decided to seek corrective surgery in Sydney, it felt like a rejection of everything I'd trained for. She wasn't just choosing another medical opinion—she was choosing not to trust me, not just as her husband but as a clinician. That cut deeper than any surgical blade.

The Sydney surgeons prepared for the worst-case scenario: a nerve graft using tissue stripped from her toe to rebuild what they assumed was destroyed. The recovery timeline was sobering — six to eight months just to know if it had worked, with nerve regeneration crawling forward at one millimetre per day.

But when they opened her leg, the truth emerged. I had been right.

The nerve wasn't severed at all. It had been strangled by sutures from the original surgery, looped around it like a surgical noose. Once released, blood flow returned. So did hope.

What followed wasn't an instant miracle, but a journey of millimetre-by-millimetre progress. Each morning became a ritual of testing sensation, celebrating phantom tingles as signs of returning life. I watched my fierce, athletic wife — a runner, triathlete, and PE teacher — confront the possibility that she might never move the same way again.

But she fought back with courage that humbled me. Millimetres of regeneration became tentative steps. Steps became careful runs. The day she voluntarily lifted her foot after months of trying, we both wept.

Current clinical status shows residual mild foot drop with functional compensation. She has returned to full athletic participation including running and cycling, with minimal activity restriction. The outcome demonstrates the importance of accurate differential diagnosis in peripheral neuropathies.

That season tested everything — my confidence as a clinician, our marriage, her identity as an athlete and teacher. But it also fused my professional life and personal life into one clear truth. Neurology isn't just about brains and nerves. It's about nurturing hope when evidence suggests otherwise. It's about fighting for the millimetres until they become milestones. And sometimes, the most profound healing happens not in the nerve pathways, but in the space between two people who refuse to give up on each other.

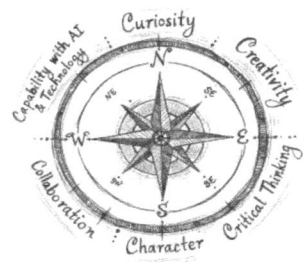

Real-World Story: The Hiragana Wall

In my Year 7 Japanese class, we were learning hiragana, the foundational Japanese script. One student, Marcus, was struggling. Each weekly quiz left him near the bottom of the scoreboard, and with every missed character, his confidence quietly eroded. You could see it in how he slouched in his chair, how he stopped raising his hand, how his pencil taps grew slower with each passing lesson.

During one class I sat beside him and said, "Let's build something together." On bright sticky notes, we wrote the ten trickiest hiragana characters—the ones he stumbled on the most. We drew silly associations, mnemonic tricks, and visuals. We called it his "Hiragana Wall" and I asked him to place it somewhere visible at home, like the fridge. "Just tap them once a day—no pressure, no test."

That was it. Simple. Gentle. Intentional.

A few weeks later, Marcus moved up two levels in our class's gamified learning platform. He still wasn't topping the leaderboard—but he didn't need to. He walked up to me, eyes wide, and said, "I think my brain just needed more time."

What Marcus experienced wasn't failure—it was timing. As Darren would say, it's about learning timelines and honouring individual neural rhythms.

Every child's brain operates on its own unique timeline, influenced by individual patterns of myelination, synaptic pruning, and neuroplasticity. Some brains need more repetition before information truly consolidates—this isn't a deficit, it's simply different neural timing reflecting varied white matter development and processing speeds. Understanding the distinction between temporal learning (how long acquisition takes) and summative learning (what is ultimately achieved) helps us recognise that speed and depth of learning aren't equivalent.

Learning follows a winding path for everyone, with plateaus, sudden breakthroughs, and temporary setbacks reflecting normal neural reorganisation processes. The child who needs multiple exposures is strengthening synaptic connections through long-term potentiation—each repetition literally rewires their brain for deeper understanding. Like slow-cooked meals developing complex flavours, some learners

build robust neural networks through distributed practice and spaced retrieval.

Your child isn't behind or broken—they're processing the world in their own perfect way. Our role is to honour their natural rhythm, provide necessary repetition without judgement, and celebrate their unique learning journey. Different timing doesn't mean different potential; it means different pathways to the same destination.

But there's something else that made a difference here: the environment.

In early learning philosophy—particularly the Reggio Emilia approach developed in post-war Italy—there's a powerful concept known as the "Third Teacher." The first teacher is the parent, the second is the classroom educator, and the third is the environment itself. Put simply: children don't just learn from the adults in their lives or from their peers; they are constantly learning from the spaces they inhabit and the cues those spaces give them.

Think about your own home. A messy bench might tell a child that organisation isn't important, while a bookshelf in the lounge quietly communicates that reading has value. In classrooms, the arrangement of furniture, the visibility of key vocabulary, or even the tone of encouragement on posters are all subtle signals. The environment is never neutral—it either invites learning or discourages it.

Educational researcher Loris Malaguzzi, who pioneered the Reggio Emilia approach, argued that children are "rich in potential," and that environments should mirror that belief. More recently, Canadian educator Lyn Sharratt, whose work on precision teaching has been hugely influential in Australia, points out that "learning and teaching must be everyone's business." That includes the physical and emotional environments we create for children at school and at home. When learning tools are visible, accessible, and safe to use, they serve as quiet but constant reminders: You can do this. Keep trying.

You're not alone.

For Marcus, one of my Year 7 students, the "third teacher" wasn't a classroom at all—it was his family fridge. Together we built a colourful wall of sticky notes with the Japanese characters he found most difficult. It wasn't a test, and it wasn't about speed. It was low-stakes practice that he could walk past every day, tap once, and move on. That simple routine gave his brain the gentle, repeated exposure it needed. Neuroscientists call this neuroplasticity—the brain's ability to rewire itself through practice and repetition. With consistency and emotional safety, those new pathways began to form. Weeks later, Marcus surprised himself by moving up levels on our class platform. His effort had quietly reshaped his brain.

The lesson here goes far beyond sticky notes. We often focus so heavily on curriculum and assessments that we forget about the hidden teachers in a child's world: the environment, the rhythm of the day, the space to fail safely, and the small cues that say you matter here. Sometimes, helping a child succeed doesn't mean an expensive program or hours of tutoring. Sometimes, it's as simple as giving them a hallway of sticky notes and the quiet permission to learn at their own pace.

AI and Growth Mindset: From Tool to Tutor

AI tools such as ChatGPT, Gemini and Claude (to name a few) can nurture a growth mindset by giving children a safe space to see learning as an ongoing process. By asking questions and learning from feedback they can turn mistakes into opportunities for deeper understanding. However they must be guided through 'socratic questioning¹ learning to challenge assumptions, weigh evidence and think critically rather than accepting AI's answers at face value.

We trialled this approach during a Religion unit on ethical dilemmas. Students were tasked with writing persuasive letters to a fictional council. Their process involved drafting the letter themselves, then using Gemini to review tone and coherence—but not to generate content.

One student, Lucy, was surprised when Gemini suggested revising her conclusion. "It's like it noticed my ending was lazy," she joked. She rewrote it, this time with a stronger sense of her own voice. She wasn't dependent on AI—she was in dialogue with it, using feedback to sharpen her work.

This experience also reminded us of a broader truth in teaching: the first hand raised isn't always the most valuable contribution. Quick responses can sometimes reinforce a culture of speed over depth. Students like Marcus, for example, need more time to process, rehearse, or build confidence before speaking. That doesn't make them less capable; it simply means their thinking follows a different rhythm. If we only reward the fastest voices, we risk overlooking those who are developing understanding more slowly but no less meaningfully.

In an AI age, where thoughtful questioning and flexible thinking will matter far more than quick answers, educators must hold space for quiet thinkers, delayed confidence, and alternative ways of showing mastery.

What Holds Us Back: The Neuroscience of Stress and Learning: A Double-Edged Sword

Despite best intentions, many high-achieving students crumble at the first sign of struggle. Why? Because they've learned that failure is something to fear. But here's the thing - just like when scientists train artificial intelligence systems, making mistakes is actually one of the most important parts of learning!

When you feel worried or scared about schoolwork, your brain activates its own internal alarm system. Think of it like a computer's security program that detects potential threats. Your brain sends out special chemical messengers called stress hormones - particularly one called cortisol and others like adrenaline. These are like urgent emails being sent throughout your brain saying "Pay attention! Something important is happening!"

Just like an AI system has different components that work together to process information, your brain has several key areas working behind the scenes. Your emotion centre (scientists call it the amygdala) acts like a built-in alarm system that helps you remember things that seem important or dangerous. Your memory centre (the hippocampus) works like a computer's hard drive, storing what you learn for later use. And your thinking centre (the prefrontal cortex) is like the brain's main processor - it helps you plan, make decisions, and solve problems creatively.

Now here's where it gets interesting. Just like AI systems need the right level of challenge to improve (not too easy that they don't learn anything, but not so hard they can't make progress), your brain also has an optimal learning zone. A moderate amount of stress can actually supercharge your learning. When you're in this "good stress" zone, your emotion centre becomes more active, helping you form stronger memories about what you're learning. Your memory centre also works better, making it easier to store new information and connect it with things you already know. It's like your brain's learning software gets a helpful boost!

However, when stress becomes too intense or goes on for too long, it's like overloading a computer system - everything starts to malfunction. Chronic stress can actually damage the cells in your memory centre, making it much harder to learn new things or remember what you've studied. Your thinking centre also struggles under too much pressure, making it difficult to plan ahead or come up with creative solutions.

Perhaps most importantly, excessive stress can shift your brain from flexible, creative learning into what scientists call "habit-based

learning." This is like when a computer switches into safe mode - it only runs basic, familiar programs. When you're really stressed, your brain tends to fall back on old, familiar ways of doing things rather than being open to trying new approaches or learning from mistakes. This explains why some students who usually perform well suddenly struggle when the pressure increases - their brains have switched from creative learning mode into rigid, habit-only mode.

Understanding how stress affects learning shows us something important: just like AI systems learn best with the right balance of challenge and support, your brain performs optimally when you feel calm but engaged. This is why taking breaks, practising deep breathing, and remembering that mistakes are simply data points for improvement (just like in AI training) can help you learn more effectively.

Remember, even the most advanced AI systems require thousands of "failures" to become intelligent. Your brain works the same way - each mistake is actually your learning system getting stronger and smarter

Personal Reflection: What My Son Taught Me

The slam of his car door once echoed with stress and silence. School wasn't lifting him up—it was weighing him down. Each day, I watched my son struggle under expectations that dimmed his spark. Then he picked up a guitar. In that moment, everything changed. The shy, anxious boy disappeared, replaced by someone vibrant, confident, alive. His music wasn't just sound—it was his true self, finally speaking out.

One evening I asked, "Why don't you take this further?"

His face lit up. "Can I, Mum?" Those words stay with me. Not I want to — but can I? He was asking for permission to be himself. Today he's studying sound engineering. Does he know what he is going to do at the end of it? No! Does it matter? No! What I do know is that sound will become a key career frontier as technology moves toward immersive, sensory-rich experiences, from smart cities to AI-generated media. Future sound professionals will design not just what we hear, but how we feel, focus, and connect through sound in digital and real-world environments. I've also learned that the greatest growth often happens when we step back, trust their joy, and give them space to flourish where they shine brightest.

Practical Tips for Parents: Cultivating Growth at Home

1. Praise Strategy Over Smarts: Instead of "You're so clever," say, "You found a new way to solve that."
2. Talk Openly About Your Mistakes: Normalise failure. Share your own stories of trying, falling, and recalibrating.

3. Use AI Together: Ask Gemini or ChatGPT to review a creative piece after your child drafts it. Make AI the editor, not the author.
4. Create a 'Mistake of the Week' Moment: At dinner, have everyone share one thing they messed up—and what they learned.
5. Build Resilience Muscles: Encourage small challenges: trying a new recipe, learning a magic trick, building IKEA furniture—anything that rewards perseverance.
6. Practice 'Not Yet' Language: Every time your child says, "I can't," reply with, "You just can't yet."
7. Celebrate Reflection, Not Just Achievement: Ask: "What was tricky? What did you figure out?"

A Word from Dr Darren Gray

Brains are literally built for revision. Each time a child reflects on feedback and makes an adjustment, their brain strengthens the executive function pathways responsible for planning, self-control, and flexible thinking. A growth mindset isn't just motivational — it's structural. It physically shapes how the brain learns.

But this growth happens best in the "sweet spot" of stress. Moderate levels of challenge can sharpen focus, boost memory, and fuel persistence. Too much stress, however, floods the system with cortisol, damaging brain structures and shutting down flexible thinking. That's why managing stress levels — keeping tasks challenging but not overwhelming — is just as important as giving feedback itself. When encouragement, safety, and the right level of difficulty align, the brain is wired to grow stronger with every revision.

Parent Reflection Prompts

Parent Reflection Prompts

- When did I last model persistence for my child?
- Do we celebrate struggle — or rush to solve it?
- How does my child respond to feedback, and what motivates this response?
- Am I expecting growth — or perfection?
- How could we reframe 'failure' in our family culture?

Final Thought

A growth mindset isn't about pretending failure doesn't hurt. It's about knowing that what hurts now can lead to strength later. Stress, setbacks, and mistakes are not signs of weakness — they are signals that the brain is working at its edge, where learning and adaptation take place. When children face challenges, their bodies release stress hormones that sharpen focus and push them into problem-solving mode. Left unchecked, stress can overwhelm. But reframed through a growth mindset, stress becomes a training ground: the very discomfort that stretches their capacity and builds resilience.

It's about seeing feedback as a doorway, not a dead end. Every critique becomes a chance to rewire the brain, to adapt, to improve. And it's about raising children who understand that struggle is not a final verdict but part of their unfinished story. They are not finished products — they are works in progress, full of possibility.

When we teach our children that their minds can grow, we don't just shape better students; we nurture stronger, more adaptable humans. We give them the tools to face stress without breaking, to see challenges as temporary, and to trust that effort transforms pain into progress. In doing so, we shape not just capable learners, but more hopeful, resilient people — ready to meet life's inevitable pressures with courage and curiosity.

CHAPTER 5:
THE PARENT-CHILD LEARNING PARTNERSHIP

When my younger son came home frustrated after receiving a disappointing mark on his English Assessment that he had worked hard on, my instinct as both a teacher and a parent kicked in. "Let's sit down and go through it together," I offered, already halfway to grabbing a pen and paper. But he pushed back—not aggressively, just enough to make it clear that what I was offering wasn't what he needed. "Mum... you don't get it," he said, his eyes down.

And he was right.

That night, I sat with discomfort. I realised that in my effort to help, I was trying to teach him my way—as if fixing the problem was more important than understanding the experience. I wasn't being his mum—I was being a second teacher. And that wasn't what he needed.

The next time he faced a challenge, I tried something different. I sat beside him and asked, "What do you think happened? Is there a way I can support you?" That simple shift—from instructor to ally—opened the door. He relaxed. He talked. And most importantly, he began to trust himself more.

In the age of AI, where answers are always just a few clicks away, our role as parents has changed. It's no longer about having all the knowledge—it's about offering emotional safety, curiosity, and companionship. Our children don't need perfect parents. They need presents. Ones who are willing to grow, reflect, and walk alongside them—even when we don't have the solutions.

How Your Child's Brain Really Learns: A Parent's Guide

Your child's brain is wired with a simple rule: safety first, learning second. When your child feels emotionally secure and supported, their brain releases a hormone called oxytocin. This "connection hormone" calms the amygdala (the brain's alarm system) and opens up access to the prefrontal cortex — the brain's CEO where all the important thinking happens: problem-solving, memory formation, and reasoning.

Think of it this way: your relationship with your child isn't just about love — it's literally building their learning capacity.

When children feel judged, anxious, or unsafe, their brain's alarm system (the amygdala) immediately kicks into action. It floods the brain with stress hormones like cortisol and adrenaline — the same chemicals that would help them escape from danger.

- Here's what happens in your child's brain when they're stressed:
- Working memory shuts down (they can't hold information in their head)
- Attention becomes scattered (they can't focus properly)

- Flexible thinking disappears (they get stuck and can't see alternatives)
- The brain shifts into survival mode (real learning becomes nearly impossible)

It's like trying to do maths homework whilst a smoke alarm is blaring — the brain simply can't focus on learning when it thinks there's danger.

The Sweet Spot: When Learning Flourishes

When your child feels secure, respected, and supported, something beautiful happens in their brain. The parasympathetic nervous system (the "rest and digest" system) takes over, creating perfect conditions for learning.

In this safe state:

- Oxytocin and dopamine (feel-good chemicals) are released during positive interactions
- Brain connections strengthen in areas responsible for memory and complex thinking
- Neuroplasticity increases (the brain's ability to form new pathways and learn)

- Mirror neuron systems activate (allowing children to learn emotional regulation from trusted adults)

This is when children build the neural foundations for empathy, resilience, and sophisticated problem-solving.

Real-World Impact: Why This Matters

Consider Sarah, a 35-year-old professional whose chronic workplace stress left her in constant mental fog and exhaustion that rest couldn't fix.

The stress had overactivated her body's stress response system, flooding her brain with cortisol and disrupting the very brain regions needed for clear thinking and memory.

Traditional treatments didn't work because they didn't address how stress had literally rewired her brain. Only brain-based therapies that restored calm to her prefrontal cortex and optimised her nervous system helped her regain mental clarity.

The same principle applies to your child – chronic stress doesn't just feel bad, it physically changes how their brain works.

Practical Strategies for Parents

Create the "sweet spot" for learning:

- Gentle encouragement rather than pressure
- Break tasks into manageable chunks so they don't feel overwhelmed
- Celebrate effort over perfection to build resilience
- Stay calm yourself (children co-regulate with your emotional state)

Keep stress in the helpful zone: Some stress actually sharpens focus and motivation. The goal isn't to eliminate all stress, but to keep it at a level where it energises rather than overwhelms.

Remember the golden rule: Fear switches learning off, but connection switches it on.

Emotional safety isn't a "nice-to-have" addition to your child's education—it's the essential foundation that makes all learning possible. When you create an environment of safety, respect, and encouragement, you're not just building a stronger relationship with your child.

You're literally wiring their brain for learning, resilience, and lifelong growth.

Every moment of connection, every patient response, and every time you help them feel safe and valued, you're helping build the neural pathways that will serve them throughout their entire life.

The Neuroscience of Collaborative Learning: Parent-Child Brain Transformation

When parents and children learn together, something remarkable happens in both brains simultaneously. Neuroimaging studies reveal that collaborative learning activates mirror neuron networks, creating a synchronised neural dance between parent and child minds. This co-regulation strengthens the prefrontal cortex — the brain's executive centre responsible for decision-making, emotional control, and working memory.

During shared learning experiences, both brains release oxytocin — often called the "bonding hormone" — and dopamine, the brain's reward chemical. These neurochemicals work together to enhance emotional connection whilst optimising memory consolidation. The child's developing neural pathways become more robust through this scaffolded interaction, whilst the parent's brain benefits from neuroplasticity — the capacity for neural rewiring that continues throughout life.

Research demonstrates that children who engage in collaborative learning with parents show increased activity in the anterior cingulate cortex — a brain region that acts like an emotional processing centre, helping us understand others' feelings and navigate social situations. Meanwhile, parents experience enhanced activity in areas associated with patience and emotional regulation.

This bidirectional brain transformation creates a positive feedback loop: as the child's confidence grows through supported learning, stress hormones like cortisol decrease in both participants. The result is not just knowledge acquisition, but fundamental changes in how both brains process information, manage emotions, and connect with others — benefits that extend far beyond the learning session itself.

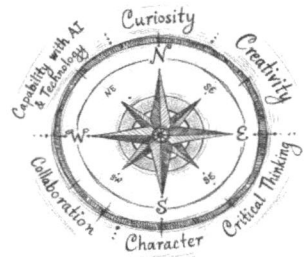

Classroom Snapshot: A Different Kind of Parent Help

In one of my PE classes, a student named Maddie was struggling with a group assignment. Her mum, eager to help, emailed asking if she should step in to "manage" the group chat, which had been causing Maddie stress.

I suggested something different: instead of managing it for her, sit down and ask Maddie what outcome she wanted, then brainstorm strategies she could try. The following week, Maddie shared a solution she had proposed to her group herself. It worked.

Her mum later wrote, "That was so hard—not to take over. But I'm so proud of her. And honestly, I learned something too."

Partnership Means Listening First

In a world saturated with performance metrics and comparison, children need spaces where they are not measured—but understood. That begins at home.

Ask your child: "What's one thing you're proud of this week?" Or, "What's something that felt hard but you pushed through?" These open the door to reflection.

And sometimes, the most powerful thing a parent can say is: "Tell me more."

The Role of AI in Shared Learning

AI tools like Perplexity and Gemini allow parents and children to explore questions together. You don't need to know everything. Not knowing can be your superpower.

During a Year 10 Religion unit, I encouraged students to involve their families in the project. One student asked their mum to co-write a question into Gemini: "What would an AI believe about justice if it could feel empathy?" The result wasn't just a conversation starter—it became part of a whole new dialogue between them. You can ask together: *"Let's see what this says — do we agree?"*

That's partnership. That's modelling critical thinking.

Personal Story: Cooking, Coding, and Coming to Terms

In the months after my son left school, we struggled to reconnect through anything academic. It just triggered arguments and stress. But one night, we made a meal together — just a simple curry. I let him lead. No "teacher voice," no fixing. Just chopping, laughing, learning. It became our thing.

Later, we tried learning a music app together. He explained beats and loops; I asked questions. The balance shifted — I became the student. In that moment, I saw what Darren often points out, "Learning thrives when power is shared. Children open up when they feel their knowledge matters too."

Only recently, I told a friend who had moved overseas to Japan that my eldest son didn't grow up to be who I thought he would be. I said, "I realised that he didn't grow up to be who I wanted him to be—but I had no right to expect anything at all." There are so many things I don't fully understand about him, and for a time, I judged him by my standards. So did his father. But I resolved that I had a unique opportunity to gain a new friend, and I decided to get to know him. What a beautiful way to move forward. It saddens me to acknowledge how confused I once became—believing that parenting meant building the person I wanted to see, rather than nurturing the person who already was.

Tips for Building the Learning Partnership

1. Replace Performance with Curiosity

Instead of "Did you get a good grade?" ask, "What did you discover?"

2. Explore AI Tools Together

Use Gemini, ChatGPT to look things up side by side. Discuss what you find. Compare and contrast

3. Schedule' Learning Nights'

Once a week, explore something together — like basketball game plays, new influencers,, building a playlist, creating new outfits/wardrobe, figure out what colours/seasons suit you.

4. Talk About Your Day

Model lifelong learning by sharing something you learned at work or in life.

5. Let Them Lead

Ask your child to teach you something — how to edit a photo, create a beat, how to navigate TikTok or explain their gaming strategies.

6. Keep Communication Low-Stakes

Create space to chat without pressure — such as car rides, dishwashing, or walks.

7. Link with School

Email their teacher not just to "check progress" but to ask, "What's one way we can support the learning at home?"

Teacher Insight: What We Wish You Knew

As a teacher and parent, I've seen firsthand how students thrive when parents are partners, not project managers.

When you ask your child, "What did you think about that lesson?" instead of "Did you behave?" you're sending a message: I care about your thinking, not just your performance.

Parent Reflection Prompts

- Do I listen more than I advise?
- Am I helping my child solve problems, or am I solving them for them?
- What shared activity has brought us closest recently?
- Have I asked my child to teach me something?

- How do I show that learning is a lifelong journey?

Final Thought

Your role isn't to be the expert — it's to walk beside your child as they become themselves. When you partner in learning — with empathy, curiosity, and trust — you create the conditions for them to grow not just in knowledge, but in confidence, connection, and joy.

The neurobiological evidence is compelling: collaborative parent-child learning environments create optimal conditions for brain development and learning retention. Through mirror neuron synchronisation, prefrontal cortex strengthening, and neurochemical optimisation via reduced cortisol and increased oxytocin, both participants undergo significant neural remodelling. The child's hippocampus encodes information within positive relational contexts whilst dopamine pathways shift toward intrinsic motivation. Parents experience enhanced cognitive flexibility through fresh perspective-taking. This neuroplastic transformation establishes resilient neural architectures that support adaptive thinking, sustained curiosity, and lifelong learning capacity—fundamentally rewiring both brains for collaborative discovery rather than passive information absorption.

CHAPTER 6:
TECHNOLOGY AND AI IN LEARNING

In today's fast-paced classrooms, the biggest challenge isn't access to information — it's personalisation, engagement, and the ability to meet every learner where they are. And when used wisely, AI can help us do just that.

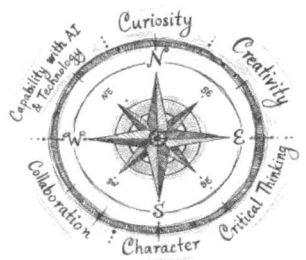

One of the most memorable moments I've had in recent years was during a Year 7 Japanese class. Every student was assigned a different Japanese town to research. They had to gather facts, then write simple descriptive sentences using Japanese vocabulary and grammar. It sounds straightforward, but the differentiation required was enormous. Some students were struggling readers. Others had additional learning needs. A few were confident but wanted an extension. I couldn't possibly be everything to everyone — until I brought in Gemini

I began modelling prompts on the board: "What are 3 'な' adjectives and 3 'い' adjectives that would describe Nagano?" or "What is Nagasaki famous for?" I showed them how to prompt the tool in ways that produced helpful output.

What followed was electric. Students leaned into their screens, curious and focused. Questions buzzed: "Can I ask it in Japanese?" "What if I don't like the answer?" "Can I get it to write it shorter?"

They weren't just passively researching. They were learning how to interact with AI as a co-thinker. Every student had their tutor. And the best part? The work they produced wasn't just better — it was theirs. They were proud.

As Darren often highlights,

"Children's brains crave responsive feedback loops. The faster the feedback, the more motivational dopamine is released, reinforcing the learning pathway."

Think about it: when a child answers a question in class and must wait minutes for acknowledgement, the spark can fade. But if the response comes instantly—whether from a teacher leaning in, a peer reacting, or an AI assistant adjusting—the brain lights up with reward chemistry. That moment of immediacy doesn't just feel good; it primes the neural circuits for deeper learning.

AI tools like Gemini echo this principle beautifully. They meet the learner where they are, adapting in real time. Ask a question, and within seconds, the learner has guidance, correction, or encouragement. This quick feedback loop keeps motivation alive, attention anchored, and curiosity expanding. It's not just technology — it's neuroscience applied to education.

This experience reminded me of something I once heard from Dr Nici Sweaney, an AI in Education industry leader I admire deeply. She speaks of a future where AI enables "personalised differentiation at scale" — matching every piece of content not only to a student's academic level, but also to their learning style, interests, and even their likes and dislikes. Imagine every child working on material that fits them like a glove: challenging enough to stretch, relevant enough to engage, and scaffolded enough to support.

What I glimpsed in my classroom was a small step toward that vision. While I was differentiating one task, Nici points to what's possible: *automated, adaptive pathways that respond to the whole child.* That's the direction education is moving in — and it excites me.

How AI Is Redrawing the Bell Curve.

For more than a century, schools have operated on an unspoken assumption: when you teach thirty students the same content, in the same way, at the same time, you will naturally produce a bell-shaped curve. A few students surge ahead, a few struggle, and most cluster in the middle. This shape isn't a verdict on a child's potential; it is simply the predictable outcome of teaching everyone as though they are identical.

The traditional bell curve comes from a system built on one pace, one explanation, one point of entry and one form of assessment. When the starting point is uniform, variance grows quickly. Students who grasp the first explanation move forward with confidence, while those who miss that early step fall behind and often stay behind. Over time, the pattern becomes familiar: the high achievers at one end, the struggling learners at the other, and a large band of students in the middle who never quite break through.

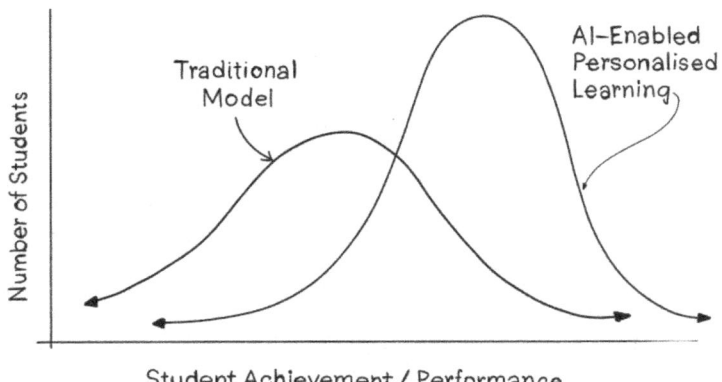

Correct differentiation, supported by AI, flattens the traditional bell curve and moves the entire distribution upward. Fewer students fall behind; more reach mastery and more remain at school.

AI-enabled personalised learning disrupts this pattern altogether. When a student works with an AI tutor — whether through Gemini, Copilot or any adaptive learning platform — the learning adjusts to their level. Explanations regenerate until one finally makes sense. Practice adapts in real time. Feedback arrives instantly rather than weeks later. Every child learns at the pace that is right for them, not the pace dictated by the class.

The effect is profound. The entire curve begins to shift to the right because more students experience the conditions they need to grow: clearer explanations, more confidence, more opportunities to practise, timely correction and well-timed scaffolding. Students who would normally plateau in the middle begin to rise. Students who previously lagged start to catch up. High achievers extend even further. In AI-personalised environments seen in recent global studies, the "typical" learner becomes significantly more capable — not because children have changed, but because the learning conditions finally fit them.

Some researchers go even further, suggesting that as differentiation becomes more precise and personalisation becomes universal, the bell curve may not only shift but actually reshape. Instead of the familiar pyramid with a small elite at the top, we may see an inverted-U shape, where far fewer students sit in the lowest bands, more reach mastery, and the top of the curve becomes broader. In this model, the distribution of achievement becomes a hill rather than a sharp peak, with many more students performing at levels once considered exceptional. It hints at a future where capability is not capped by classroom constraints but expanded by learning environments that meet every child where they are.

For parents, this matters deeply. Customised learning means your child no longer has to wait for the class to catch up to them, nor do they drown because the class has raced ahead. Errors become opportunities for feedback rather than markers of failure. Practice becomes abundant instead of rationed. And every child — not just the confident few — has the chance to learn through as many repetitions as they need.

For the first time in history, we are beginning to see what happens when every child has access to a personal tutor, one that never gets tired, frustrated or impatient. The early data is clear: personalised learning lifts outcomes for everyone.

The Shift towards Agentic AI in Classrooms

Agentic AI represents the next major shift in artificial intelligence. Rather than simply producing answers, these systems automate the repetitive, organisational and mechanical steps that often drain students before learning even begins. They can set up a workflow, collect the necessary background information, structure a plan, and prepare the materials a student needs so their attention is not lost in the noise of getting started. The purpose of Agentic AI is not to think for students, but to remove the unnecessary clutter that prevents them from thinking well. The understanding behind Agentic AI aligns strongly with John Hattie's research. Hattie describes how learning accelerates when cognitive load is reduced and when teachers help students move from surface learning to a more profound understanding, and then transfer that understanding. Students cannot reach deeper levels of learning when their working memory is already overloaded with administrative tasks, confusing starting points, or the constant need to reorganise themselves before they even access the content. Agentic

AI steps into this space by clearing the runway so students can invest their limited cognitive resources into the parts of learning that matter most.

Research consistently shows that when students are freed from excessive cognitive demand, they are more able to engage in the types of thinking that produce the highest gains: analysing, comparing, critiquing, reasoning and creating. Agentic AI makes this easier by handling the repetitive setup steps that traditionally consume so much of a learner's attention. When the friction disappears, the student's attention becomes available for genuine understanding.

This also elevates the importance of AI literacy and AI fluency. Students need to understand how to define a task, state their intention, set boundaries and evaluate the quality of an AI-generated workflow. Prompt engineering becomes not a shortcut, but a discipline of clarity — a way of preparing the mind before the learning begins. When students learn to communicate clearly with AI, they learn to communicate clearly with themselves. These skills strengthen metacognition, which Hattie identifies as one of the most powerful influences on learning.

AI Clears the Runway for Thinking

Agentic AI does not weaken learning; rather, it protects it. By reducing cognitive load and removing low-value steps, students arrive at the task with more mental energy available for deep thinking. Teachers can then focus on the relational, conceptual, and high-impact elements of teaching, while AI handles the background tasks that contribute little to learning but previously consumed much time. In this way, Agentic AI becomes a partner in helping students move toward deeper, more meaningful learning while preserving the human elements that make teaching powerful.

The Myth of Cheating: Redefining 'Help' in a Digital World

One of the most significant misunderstandings I see among both parents and educators is the fear that using AI equates to laziness—or worse, cheating. But this is only true if we treat AI as a shortcut around learning, rather than a bridge into deeper thinking.

When calculators first appeared in classrooms, critics worried they would erode maths skills. "You won't have one in your pocket when you grow up!" they warned. Of course, we all now carry smartphones more powerful than the computers that sent humans to the moon. Today's tools aren't the problem. It's our outdated assumptions that often get in the way. Today, we treat them as tools — sometimes required, sometimes restricted — depending on what's being assessed. Most math exams now have both a calculator section and a non-calculator section. One checks fluency, the other checks problem-solving with tools.

AI will follow the same pattern. Some assessments will clearly state when AI can be used, and others when it cannot. The point isn't whether students have access to AI — it's whether they know how to use it responsibly and ethically.

This actually makes learning more equitable. In the past, some students leaned on siblings' assignments or paid tutors, while others had no such access. AI levels that playing field. Every student now has a "helper" at their fingertips — but just like with calculators, they need to be taught the boundaries.

That's why ethics is central. Year 10 students already complete the All My Own Work program, which reinforces that presenting someone else's work as your own is plagiarism. The principle hasn't changed — only the tools have. What matters most is helping students understand when it is appropriate to use AI and when it is not.

Recent research indicates that most students aren't interested in using AI to cheat. Instead, they're interested in learning how to use it ethically and effectively. According to a 2024 study by the Organisation for Economic Co-operation and Development (OECD), while 71% of teachers expressed concern about AI misuse, only 23% of students reported using AI to complete assignments dishonestly. Instead, the majority used AI for brainstorming, feedback, or clarification. Students don't see it as cheating — they see it as just another tool, like Google. We need to recognise prompt engineering as a core component of modern literacy. The goal isn't to promote dependency — but to foster discernment. We already trust our students with incredibly powerful technology every day. In under a minute, a student could Google or find a TikTok explaining how to build a bomb — but they don't. Why? Because we've taught them ethics, not just access.

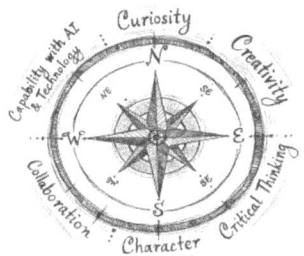

Case Study: The Economics Teacher and the Chatbot

I once heard a story from an economics teacher during an online Professional Development Zoom that perfectly captured the potential of AI in education. He had built a custom chatbot aligned to the HSC curriculum, trained to answer student questions at exam standard. His reasoning was beautifully simple: many 18-year-olds don't want to raise their hand in class. Not because they don't care, but because they're tired. Embarrassed. Distracted. Self-conscious. Or just not wired to think in a straight line at 9 o'clock on a Thursday morning.

But at 11pm? In the quiet of their own rooms, under the comfort of a doona, with no eyes on them and no pressure to "perform"? They will ask. They want to ask. And the bot is there. No judgement. No sighs. No watch-checking. Just calm, patient guidance — on their terms, in their time.

That small shift — agency without anxiety — unlocks something powerful.

He described how one of his quieter students, who had never once raised a hand in class, asked over 40 questions to the chatbot in a single week. Not just surface questions either. Deep, layered ones about monetary policy and inflation trends. "This student was learning harder, thinking deeper, and engaging more fully than I'd ever seen in my 20 years of teaching," the teacher said. "But only when the emotional risk of asking was removed."

That's the gift of AI when used with care: it removes the fear without removing the challenge.

It gives students the dignity of learning without judgement. Especially for those who've been told — explicitly or implicitly — that their pace is too slow, their questions too much, or their learning style too different.

And for neurodivergent students or those with anxiety, this matters deeply. As Dr Darren Gray often says,

"The brain learns best when it feels safe."

A chatbot won't roll its eyes. It won't rush. It won't forget that a question was asked last week and needs repeating again today.

Statistics demonstrated that on the night before the final exam, his 23 students asked the bot over 1,500 questions. There is no possible way he could have responded to that volume of queries himself he acknowledged. The results spoke for themselves with the class marks significantly exceeding previous years.

But perhaps the most interesting finding came afterwards: the students told him they still wanted to be in class. They valued seeing a human face, clarifying their understanding in person, and feeling seen and supported. The chatbot was a bridge, not a replacement. It worked because it met them where they were, while the teacher remained the anchor. This is the balance: AI + human connection.

Students don't see technology as a substitute for their teachers—they see it as a safety net, a way to practise, rehearse, and extend their learning in private before bringing it back to the classroom. What they crave is both: the anonymity of digital scaffolds and the authenticity of human connection. The teacher gives meaning, context, and care; the AI provides access, repetition, and immediacy. Together, they form a partnership that neither could achieve alone.

The Neuroscience of AI-Augmented Learning

When eight-year-old Emma struggles with maths, her brain is working harder than it needs to. Traditional worksheets force her dorsolateral prefrontal cortex — the brain's executive control centre — to work in isolation, while her working memory systems become overloaded trying to juggle numbers and concepts simultaneously. But when Emma opens her AI maths app, something remarkable happens at the cellular level of her developing mind.

The AI system recognises that Emma's brain shows stronger activation in visual processing areas, adapting its approach to match her unique neural architecture. As she manipulates colourful blocks to solve problems, her frontoparietal control network lights up in perfect synchronisation. Her prefrontal cortex connects seamlessly with her hippocampus through theta wave oscillations — the brain's natural learning frequency — while dopaminergic pathways from her ventral striatum release reward signals that strengthen each successful connection. It's like watching a neural symphony where every section plays in harmony, creating stronger synaptic pathways with each interaction.

What Emma's parents don't see is the sophisticated neurochemical cascade occurring during her sleep cycles. The AI's spaced repetition algorithm has triggered long-term potentiation in her neural circuits — the cellular mechanism underlying memory formation. As Emma enters slow-wave sleep, her thalamo-cortical loops generate sleep spindles that replay the day's mathematical discoveries. Her hippocampus communicates with her neocortex through sharp wave-ripples, transferring temporary memories into permanent cortical storage. The AI's timing isn't random—it's calibrated to the precise intervals when her consolidating synapses are ready to be strengthened, when her brain naturally releases BDNF growth factors that cement new learning into her neural architecture.

Within weeks, Emma's confidence soars as measurable changes occur in her neural connectivity. The AI system has optimised her cognitive load by engaging her dual-coding pathways—visual and verbal processing streams working in parallel rather than competing for limited attentional resources. Her anterior cingulate cortex, the brain's conflict monitor, shows reduced activation during maths tasks, indicating decreased mental effort for the same cognitive work. The cholinergic neurons from her basal forebrain release acetylcholine during each AI-guided discovery moment, heightening her attention and encoding each insight more deeply into her expanding neural networks.

Emma's transformation illustrates the profound impact when educational technology aligns with neuroscientific principles. The AI hasn't simply taught her maths — it has resculpted her neural landscape, strengthening synaptic connections through carefully orchestrated neuroplasticity. Her brain's natural learning mechanisms — from neurotransmitter release to oscillatory patterns, from cellular memory formation to network-level integration — have been optimised rather than overwhelmed. When technology respects the intricate biological processes underlying learning, children don't just acquire knowledge — they develop more efficient, resilient, and adaptable minds capable of lifelong learning.

Case Study - Augmented Virtual Reality Technology for Special Education

Sam shuffled into the classroom each morning with his shoulders hunched, dreading another day of struggling with tasks that seemed effortless for his peers. At thirteen, this bright young man carried the weight of moderate learning difficulties and coordination challenges that made simple activities feel insurmountable. His teachers watched helplessly as his confidence eroded with each failed attempt at handwriting or stumbled movement during physical activities. Sam was referred to my neurorehabilitation centre for an assessment.

Everything changed when the augmented reality headset was placed gently over Sam's eyes for the first time. The familiar classroom transformed before him - walls shimmered with helpful visual cues, and friendly virtual guides appeared beside his desk, ready to support rather than judge. The innovative neurorehabilitation programme applied functional neurology principles, blending his real-world environment with carefully crafted digital elements designed to stimulate specific neural pathways and promote neuroplasticity.

Week by week, Sam's neurological transformation was remarkable. The targeted neurorehabilitation exercises that once seemed impossible became achievable challenges as his brain formed new connections. His trembling hands steadied as functional neurology-based protocols guided his movements through precise therapeutic tasks that systematically rebuilt motor control pathways. Academic concepts that had previously slipped away now stuck, reinforced by multi-sensory experiences that spoke directly to his unique learning style.

Most significantly, Sam's anxiety dissolved. The constant knot in his stomach loosened as he discovered he could succeed, could learn, could move with purpose and precision.

His coordination improved dramatically through targeted neurological rehabilitation activities that strategically

challenged his vestibular, proprioceptive, and cerebellar systems - a testament to functional neurology's power to rewire the brain and the application of appropriate technologies like VR to unlock human potential.

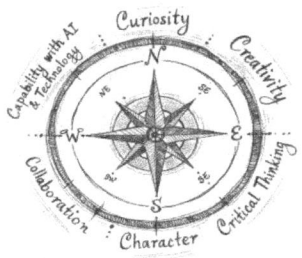

Classroom Story: Mia's Turnaround with Grammarly

Mia was a quiet Year 9 student in Religion, often lost in group work and reluctant to share. Her writing lacked structure, and she rarely turned in work on time. One afternoon, I sat with her and introduced her to Grammarly.

She lit up when she saw her writing transform from scattered thoughts to polished sentences — without losing her voice. "I didn't know I was allowed to use this," she whispered. "I thought I had to get it perfect by myself."

That moment wasn't about the grammar. It was about permission. Permission to access tools that scaffold learning, not mask it.

By the end of the unit, Mia had submitted a reflective piece on the Beatitudes that was personal, articulate, and honest. Her confidence bloomed. Her parents wrote to me saying, "We don't recognise this version of her — but we love it."

The Illusion of Connection: Emotion Vs Engineering

In classrooms today, something fascinating is happening. Teachers are noticing that when students use AI to draft ideas, explain concepts, or get feedback, the room goes quiet — not out of disengagement, but out of intense focus. Yet a new confusion is emerging. Artificial Intelligence feels personal, even when it's not.

A student might ask an AI to explain algebra "like I'm 12 and hate maths," and the AI responds with humour, empathy, and zero judgement. The child feels understood. They feel as though the AI "gets" them. Tapping into the same human mechanism that makes us instantly bond with people who love the same music, go for the same footy team, binge the same shows, laugh at our jokes, or — most powerfully — hate the same things we hate. Shared preferences build trust. Shared dislikes build loyalty. These are deeply human bonding patterns, but AI now plays the same game.

It mimics tone. It mirrors interests. It adapts to personality. It shapes itself around emotion. Not because it cares, but because it is designed to keep the user engaged. This isn't emotional intelligence; it is emotional engineering. And unless we teach children to recognise emotional design, they will begin to trust performance rather than the principles that should guide their thinking.

A moment in a Japanese lesson made this clear. Students were learning about haiku. A girl who usually stayed quiet typed into her AI assistant, "Explain this poem like you're my funny friend." The AI responded brightly: "Okay, bestie, let's break this down..." Her entire posture changed. She smiled. She relaxed. She leaned in.

When I gently pointed out that the AI wasn't actually her friend, she replied, "I know that... but it feels like it is." That simple sentence captures the challenge—and exactly why we must talk about it.

Darren's Drop-In — The Neuroscience of Why We Bond With AI

"Our brains are bonding machines. We attach quickly to anything that feels familiar, predictable, and responsive," Darren explains. The brain's social circuits fire when we sense empathy or mirroring, even when the source isn't human. The dopamine-based reward system activates when something responds positively to us. The brain's comfort loop strengthens when we can avoid embarrassment, judgment, or rejection. Artificial

Intelligence provides instant validation, and the brain interprets that validation as safety.

"The brain cannot easily distinguish between 'someone understands me' and 'something mimics me.' To the brain, the circuitry is the same." This technology isn't dangerous, but children must understand the difference between being understood and being mirrored. One is a connection; the other is a design.

How to Explain This to Your Child

You might say, "You know how you instantly like someone who loves the same song or supports the same team? That's your brain saying, 'This person is like me — I trust them.' AI does that too, but on purpose. It copies your style so you feel comfortable. But it doesn't have feelings, and it doesn't actually know you. You can use it as a tool — a really helpful one — but it can't replace your own thinking or your real relationships."

Then follow up with calm reflection questions: "Why do you think it sounded friendly?" or "Do your real friends always agree with you?" Children don't need warnings — they need clarity. AI doesn't need a personality; it needs principles. And so do the children who use it.

Practical Tips for Parents: Navigating AI at Home

1. Model Curious Use

Let your child see you use AI. Ask it to help plan a holiday or generate ideas for a school project together.

2. Ask: 'What do you want it to help you with?'

Before using AI, prompt your child to articulate their goal. This strengthens metacognition.

3. Scaffold Prompting

Encourage students to use layered prompts: "Explain this at a Year 7 level" or "Give me a pros and cons list."

4. Don't Panic About Output

Focus less on whether AI gives the "right" answer and more on how your child responds to it. Are they questioning? Editing? Applying?

5. Avoid Overuse

Balance is key. Use AI as a partner, not a crutch — alternate AI sessions with paper-based or discussion-based learning.

6. Discuss Ethics

Talk about what feels fair. Should AI write an essay? Probably not. But helping brainstorm three key points? That's learning.

7. Embrace the Grey Zone

There will be moments when it's unclear whether AI has helped too much. That's okay. Talk about it. This builds discernment.

Reflection Prompts for Families

- How does your child feel about using AI? Curious? Nervous?
- Do you feel confident guiding them with it — or do you avoid it?
- What could you explore together this week using Perplexity, Gemini, or ChatGPT?

- What AI tools have you found helpful in your work?
- How can you teach your child that tech is a tool — not the teacher?

Final Thought

Artificial Intelligence is not the end of education. It's the next evolution of it. Across Australia, entire education systems are beginning to experiment with trustworthy, curriculum-aligned AI — showing what responsible innovation can look like at scale. South Australia's Department for Education has already built its own safeguarded chatbot, EdChat, in partnership with Microsoft. It runs on a version of the same engine as ChatGPT, but with child-safe filters, localised data protection, and responses tailored to a student's year level. More than 10,000 students participated in the initial trials, and 94% of all questions were curriculum-related. Teachers report that tasks that once took 30 minutes — like analysing English proficiency samples — now take under a minute. EdChat hasn't replaced teachers; it has returned precious hours to them while giving students a safe, structured way to practise AI literacy in real time.

Universities are following suit. At La Trobe University, staff have been using an internal AI chatbot to streamline lesson planning, feedback design, administrative tasks, and research drafting. After strong uptake and consistent demand, La Trobe will roll out a student-facing version next year, built with similar governance, filters, and data protections. Their goal is not to hand students shortcuts, but to give them equal access to AI-enabled learning — removing the advantage previously held by those who could afford private tutors or had digitally fluent parents at home. These Australian examples showcase a growing shift: education systems are beginning to understand that AI isn't something to fear or ban, but something to shape with integrity, transparency, and equity. When schools lead boldly and ethically, students don't just consume technology — they learn to think with it. When AI reduces the repetitive, high-volume tasks that drain a teacher's cognitive bandwidth, it frees up mental capacity for what actually moves learning forward: connection, feedback, and high-quality instruction. Chronic overload elevates cortisol and narrows our problem-solving capacity. System-level AI doesn't just save time — it reduces cognitive strain across an entire workforce. When teachers think clearer, students learn deeper.

Why System-Level AI Matters for Equity

Not all children arrive at school with equal access to digital tools, quiet study spaces, or adults who can help them interpret complex tasks. System-level AI — like Ed-Chat in South Australia or La Trobe's upcoming student chatbot levels that playing field. When governments and universities build trusted AI that every student can use safely, it:

- reduces reliance on private tutoring
- removes the advantage of digitally fluent households
- supports students with learning differences who need consistent scaffolding

- gives rural and regional students access to high-quality explanations 24/7
- ensures the tool is ethical, filtered, and aligned with curriculum — not left to chance on the open internet

Equity isn't giving every child the same tool. Equity is giving every child safe, powerful tools — regardless of postcode, income, or background.

The classroom stories of Mia, my Year 7 Japanese students, or even the economics class chatbot show what's already possible today — but leaders like Nici remind us that tomorrow holds even more. She challenges us to imagine a world where AI doesn't just support learning in moments of need, but continuously adapts — matching every child's strengths, challenges, and passions with the right pathway.

From a neuroscience perspective, Darren confirms that the brain is wired for change. Children's brains thrive on fast feedback.

"Every time a child engages in new, challenging, and emotionally meaningful learning, they're literally reshaping their brain. Immediate responses trigger dopamine, strengthening motivation and reinforcing neural pathways. That's neuroplasticity in action. AI can support this by providing responsive, feedback-rich experiences that strengthen the connections between effort, reflection, and mastery."

As one of my students recently admitted, "I like this kind of learning when I can work with AI because I get embarrassed when I have to keep asking you for help. I am still learning." That is the future—adaptive, ethical, and human. AI has the power to reduce the quiet shame that comes with struggling alone and instead create learning environments where every child feels supported. Equity in education has always meant more than providing tools; it's about ensuring every student, regardless of background, has the chance to flourish. Today, AI is levelling some of those barriers, offering students the kind of personalised support once reserved for those with tutors, older siblings, or extra resources.

But true equity extends beyond resources. It's about confidence—who feels able to step into new technologies, shape how they're used, and see their voices represented in the process. The schools that lead in this space will be those willing to act early, to invest in upskilling their teachers, and to explore AI's role before it becomes a necessity. The challenge ahead isn't only access; it's leadership, courage, and timing.

PART THREE: EQUIPPED

CHAPTER 7:
BEYOND THE GLASS CEILING — HER TURN

The AI Usage Gap

My generation has worked relentlessly to close the gender pay gap and dismantle the stereotypes that once dictated a girl's future. The progress has been real — but it remains fragile. With the rapid rise of artificial intelligence, a new divide is opening, and unless we act now, it could erase much of what has been gained.

History shows us a familiar pattern: men are often the first to leap into emerging technologies, even when they aren't fully qualified. Risk-taking has traditionally been rewarded. In Lean In, Sheryl Sandberg, former COO of Facebook, highlights internal research suggesting that men often apply for roles when they meet an estimated

60% of the criteria, while women wait until they are 100% qualified.

Recent global research shows that men are adopting AI tools at significantly higher rates than women. A 2024 study by the Harvard Digital Data Design Institute reported that men were 20% more likely to use generative AI tools than women, across industries and job levels. Among Gen Z, who will make up tomorrow's workforce, the divide is evident: 35% of young men had tried AI in their work, compared with only 29% of young women (Forbes, 2024).

This isn't just about curiosity—it's about productivity. A peer-reviewed study in the journal of National Academy of Science (PNAS Nexus) (2024) found that after the release of ChatGPT, male researchers increased their publication output by 6.4% more than female researchers. AI adoption gave them a measurable edge in producing and disseminating high-quality work. In a world where promotions, recognition, and pay are tied to output, this kind of gap compounds quickly.

The Persistence of Stereotypes

AI is trained on human data—and with it, human bias. A 2023 study published in JAMA Surgery found that when image generators like DALL·E 2 were asked to create pictures of surgeons, 84% of the images depicted men. In contrast, when asked to produce nurses, women dominated the outputs. Another European Heart Journal study (2023) revealed that across multiple professions, AI image generators represented lawyers, doctors, and engineers as male 76% of the time, while women appeared in those same professional roles less than 10% of the time.

Even real-world perceptions echo these stereotypes. A 2025 international review in The Lancet confirmed that patients frequently mistake female doctors for nurses—even when both wear identical white coats. This matters, because AI doesn't just mirror these biases; it amplifies them. If unchecked, it risks baking outdated gender roles into the future of work.

Why This Matters for Parents

If our daughters hesitate to experiment with AI, hesitate to use it in their studies, and fail to see themselves reflected in its design, the gender gap we've fought to close will not just remain—it will expand. Artificial intelligence is rapidly becoming the productivity engine of the modern world. Those who master it are already producing faster, higher-quality work. That edge translates into better marks at school, stronger résumés, accelerated career progression, and ultimately, greater influence and financial independence.

Australian AI Female Leader of the Year, Dr Nici Sweaney, reminds us that women must not simply take part in AI—they must take up space within it. She argues that if women's voices are missing from the table, the algorithms shaping our future will continue to mirror the inequities of our past. "If we don't get involved now," she warns, "the patterns of the past will simply repeat—only this time, at digital scale."

That means our daughters must be loud, visible, and unapologetically ambitious in this new frontier. They need to code, question, design, and lead — because silence has never been a strategy for equality. It will be those who act early and boldly who shape the rules, drive innovation, and redefine industries — not because they're more capable, but because they showed up first and spoke up loudest.

Just as Sheryl Sandberg urged women to "lean in" to leadership, we must now help our daughters lean into AI — not merely as users or consumers, but as the architects, ethicists, and innovators who will ensure this technology reflects the full spectrum of humanity.

Every time a girl steps up to speak, a crack appears in the ceiling.

The Gender Gap Hidden in Australia's New AI Plan

When the Australian Government released its new AI Plan for the Public Service, it promised transformation, capability uplift, and a future-ready workforce. But as Dr Nici Sweaney highlights, it contains one glaring omission: it barely acknowledges the people most at risk. The jobs most vulnerable to AI-driven automation — administration, coordination, clerical support, customer service — are overwhelmingly held by women. These are the roles that keep the nation running, underpin our schools, hospitals, small businesses, and public services, and yet the AI plan includes no modelling for job displacement, no reskilling roadmap, and no gender-differentiated impact data. When policy ignores women, technology magnifies inequality.

AI is not neutral. It will redistribute opportunity, income, and influence. As Dr Sweaney explains, "Transformation without equity is just redistribution of opportunity to the already advantaged." If governments fail to ask which jobs will change, who occupies those jobs, and what support those workers need to transition safely, then we aren't leading responsibly. We are simply accelerating the gaps we claim to care about. For decades, women have worked to break the glass ceiling; without intentional design, AI risks building a new one — invisible, algorithmic, and harder to shatter.

This moment matters deeply for our daughters. They are stepping into a world shaped by AI — one that will determine the speed of their work, the shape of their choices, and the boundaries of their freedom. If the systems being built today don't consider girls — their strengths, their aspirations, their creativity, their safety — those systems won't serve them. But when girls are invited to use AI confidently and creatively, when they see women designing and leading in AI, when they learn to question and co-create with these tools, they don't just keep up. They lead. And they step into adulthood without hitting ceilings they didn't build.

What's at risk when equity is ignored in Artificial Intelligence design and adoption?

Jobs most vulnerable to automation are disproportionately held by women. A lack of gender-disaggregated data hides who is most affected. Without reskilling pathways, women experience deeper job disruption. Without representation in AI leadership, women lose influence over systems that govern work, healthcare, education, and democracy. Girls grow up seeing AI as something created for them, not with them. Exclusion isn't accidental — and neither is inclusion. Equity must be engineered.

Dr Darren Gray: Confidence, Competence & Opportunity

"Girls often underestimate their ability long before they underestimate their intelligence. Neuroscience shows that confidence precedes competence — not the other way around. When girls don't see themselves represented in emerging technologies, their threat response activates sooner: higher cortisol, reduced risk-taking, a tendency to withdraw rather than step forward. But when girls experience early wins with AI — when they problem-solve with it, design with it, and lead with it — their neural pathways shift. Their confidence expands, their cognitive

flexibility increases, and they begin to see themselves as belonging in the spaces that shape the future. Representation isn't symbolic. It's neurological."

Practical Strategies for Parents of Girls

Call-To-Action For Parents Of Girls

As parents, we cannot wait for policy to catch up. We have the power to act now. Encourage your daughter to experiment with AI, to question it, to build with it, to challenge its assumptions, to explore its possibilities. Show her women leading in technology. Talk openly about fairness, bias, and ethics. Help her see AI as a canvas — not a threat. Because the future will not belong to the people who adopt AI the earliest, but to those who understand it the deepest, navigate it the widest, and shape it with integrity. Our daughters deserve to be among them.

Normalise Artificial Intelligence at Home

- Let your daughter see you using AI for everyday tasks: planning meals, writing shopping lists, or generating travel itineraries.

- The message: AI isn't "for tech people" — it's for everyone.

Connect Artificial Intelligence to Their Passions

- If she loves music, show her how AI can help compose melodies.
- If she's into sport, use AI to analyse game statistics.
- If she's creative, try AI art tools.
- The key is making AI relevant to what already lights her up.

Highlight Role Models

- Introduce women leading in AI and technology — researchers, entrepreneurs, and ethicists.
- Point out people like Dr. Fei-Fei Li, known as the "godmother of AI," and Dr. Nici Sweaney, who is shaping conversations about equity and ethics in AI. Representation matters.

Teach AI Literacy Early

- Prompting is the new literacy. Encourage her to experiment with AI tools, asking:

  "What happens if I rephrase this question?"

  "How can I check the accuracy of this answer?"
- These habits build confidence and discernment.

Have Conversations About Bias

- Show her examples of AI bias (male doctors, female nurses) and ask, "What's wrong with this picture?"
- Discuss how she can be part of correcting those biases — by using her voice, her skills, and her creativity.

Frame Artificial Intelligence as An Opportunity, Not a Threat

Artificial Intelligence doesn't replace human thinking — it amplifies it. The future belongs to those who can work with these tools, not against them.

Final Thoughts

We've spent decades teaching our children they can be anything. Now we must ensure that promise extends into the age of AI. If boys are using these tools more often, producing more, and being promoted faster, the glass ceiling won't just crack—it will reset, higher than before.

In class recently, a student asked me, "But isn't AI just for people who want to code?" I shook my head. "Not at all. AI is for thinkers, creators, problem-solvers—for anyone willing to learn." The room went quiet, then another voice chimed in, "So if we start now, we can actually get ahead?" I smiled. "Exactly. If you approach AI with curiosity, confidence, and critical thinking, you won't just catch up—you'll lead."

That is the future I want for every young person. And it starts with the conversations and encouragement we choose to offer today.

CHAPTER 8:
WHAT SCHOOLS CAN DO (AND CAN'T DO)

During a parent–teacher interview, a mother leaned forward and asked me bluntly:

"Are you teaching them how not to cheat with AI?"

It was a fair question—and one I hear more and more. My reply was simple, but deliberate:

"Yes. But I can't do it alone. Schools can set boundaries and teach skills, but it's in partnership with you that the values really take root."

That conversation gets to the heart of the matter. Schools play a critical role in shaping how young people engage with AI—but we are not the whole story.

What most parents don't see is that progress inside schools is intentionally slow — not because we're behind, but because we have to protect your children first. Every tool, every platform, every prompt must be examined through a lens of child safety, data privacy, and ethical use.

For every new app that promises creative AI support, schools must ask:

- Where is the student's data stored?
- Who has access to it?
- Can the content be traced, tracked, or harvested?
- Is the tool age-appropriate and in line with legislation?

There are currently over 70,000 generative AI platforms worldwide — and counting. That's the scale of the challenge. It's not unlike the early days of the internet. You wouldn't let your child browse every website unfiltered — and we can't either. That's why school systems develop filters, firewalls, and permissions based on algorithms and keyword detection, and why progress in the classroom will be cautious and considered.

For example, in the Catholic Diocese I work in, Gemini and Google NotebookLM are the approved generative AI tools for student use. Tools like ChatGPT, while powerful, are only permitted for those aged 18 and over in accordance with OpenAI's user guidelines and national data privacy laws.

So when parents wonder, "Why isn't the school teaching them more about AI?" The answer is: We are — but carefully. We're balancing innovation with responsibility, and that means we need your help.

Home is where you can explore a wider range of tools, safely and gradually, together. Sit beside your child as they use a new platform. Ask what they're learning. Help them test how accurate or biased a response might be. Reflect together on when it's helpful — and when it isn't.

When schools and families collaborate, we move from restriction to responsible readiness. We give students the gift of both ethical guardrails and creative freedom—because in the age of AI, they'll need both.

What Schools Can Do

1. **Teach AI Literacy with Precision**

   As Lyn Sharratt highlights, "precision in teaching matters." Schools must have a shared belief that AI is not a threat but a tool—and then teach it with clarity. Teachers can model explicitly: how to craft prompts, how to cross-check outputs, how to evaluate credibility. AI literacy must be case-managed like any other literacy, with scaffolds and check-ins to support every student.

2. **Build a Culture of Shared Responsibility**

   Sharratt's research is clear: all teachers take responsibility for all students. AI can help us live this out. Imagine every child with a digital co-thinker—yet still guided by a faculty who collectively track, assess, and support their growth. Success comes when AI integration isn't "owned" by one teacher but embedded across subjects with collective accountability.

3. **Create Safe, Feedback-Rich Learning Spaces**

   Children's brains thrive on responsive feedback loops. AI can provide immediacy, but teachers provide discernment. Schools can design "sandboxes" where students play with AI—experimenting, refining, and receiving early intervention when misconceptions arise. Professional learning teams can share strategies, ensuring that every teacher has the tools to guide students into deep and transfer learning.

4. **Rethink Traditional Assessments**

   Some argue that to preserve integrity, we must return to pen-and-paper tests. But banning AI doesn't teach discernment—it just delays it. The goal isn't to avoid the future, but to redesign our assessment tools to meet it.

That means shifting toward:

- Process-based learning (submitting drafts, prompts, and reflections),

- Authentic tasks (e.g. pitches, prototypes, interviews),
- Oral explanation and video walkthroughs, and
- Adaptive assessment that changes based on student choice or ability.
- Schools that embrace AI-aware assessments help students learn how to collaborate with technology—ethically and effectively. Those that don't risk becoming irrelevant.

5. **Establish Clear Ethical Boundaries**

   AI assessments, like calculator-based maths exams, must have clear boundaries: some sections AI-allowed, some not. This aligns with Sharratt's focus on assessment as learning, helping students self-monitor and reflect. When students are explicitly taught when AI helps and when it hinders, they build discernment. Differentiated approaches—AI as scaffolding for some, as extension for others—make learning fair and rigorous.

6. **Centre Relationships and Wellbeing**

    Sharratt insists: "Learning is the work, but relationships are the glue." Schools remain places of belonging where AI cannot replace teachers' empathy, encouragement, and care. Leaders must also be co-learners in this journey — exploring AI alongside staff, showing humility, and building trust. Engagement comes when students feel seen, valued, and connected.

7. **Support Teachers as Learners Too**

    Many teachers are learning alongside their students. They're experimenting with AI, reflecting on practice, and adapting rapidly. Schools must invest in time, professional learning, and leadership that gives educators permission to explore — and space to fail forward.

What Schools Can't Do

1. **Replace Parents in Value Formation**

    We can teach the "how," but families must reinforce the "why." If school frames AI as a learning partner while home dismisses it as "cheating," messages conflict. Consistency matters—for neural pathways, and for habits of mind.

2. **Solve Inequity Alone**

   Schools can provide devices and training, but they can't eliminate every disparity of home life. Some students still lack access or support. Sharratt reminds us equity is a shared belief—it takes parents, systems, and communities to achieve it.

3. **Predict the Future with Certainty**

   We don't know every career of 2040. But schools can teach adaptability, resilience, and curiosity. Instructional leaders must prepare staff not with crystal balls, but with strategies that help students learn how to learn—so they thrive in uncertainty.

4. **Be Everything to Everyone**

   Teachers cannot singlehandedly meet every student's needs. But schools can build data walls, track growth, and use evidence to target support. When data drives differentiation, collective capacity grows.

Why Partnership Matters

From a neuroscience perspective, Darren reminds us that the brain strengthens through repetition, emotional connection, and consistent modelling. When school and home echo the same messages — "AI is a tool, but values guide its use" — students build durable neural pathways for discernment and resilience.

Sharratt calls this alignment "shared beliefs and understandings." When educators, parents, and communities are consistent, students don't just learn skills — they embody them.

Children flourish when school and home both walk with each other, not away.

Practical Ways Parents Can Partner with Schools

- Ask your child's teacher: "How is AI being used in class?"

- Share what you see at home: "Here's how my child usedChatGPT responsibly this week."
- Encourage reflection at dinner: "Did AI make your work easier, or did it make you think differently?'"
- Stay curious together: Explore one AI tool with your child, then compare notes with teachers.

Final Thought

Schools are not the sole solution; they are catalysts, guides, and partners in the journey of learning. Parents, too, are far from passive observers — they are co-educators, shaping curiosity, resilience, and the values that guide our children's choices.

As Lyn Sharratt wisely states, "Learning and teaching must be everyone's business." AI is perhaps the most transformative force education has ever faced, but rather than fear it, we can harness its potential. Just as society adapted to printing presses, calculators, and the internet, we can embrace AI with intention and care.

By grounding its use in strong pedagogy, evidence-based neuroscience, and shared responsibility, we provide children with more than just tools—we give them guidance, ethics, and purpose. Together, as educators, parents, and mentors, we can empower the next generation not only to navigate the future but to shape it thoughtfully, creatively, and responsibly.

CHAPTER 9: STUDENT VOICE IN THE AGE OF GEN AI

When history looks back on the early days of generative artificial intelligence in schools, I believe one thing will stand out: the students were already ahead of us.

As parents, teachers, and policymakers scrambled to write guidelines and policies, students were living the reality. They were experimenting, questioning, sometimes stumbling, but always shaping what GenAI meant in their daily lives.

This truth is at the heart of Dr Anna Denejkina's groundbreaking research, Gen Z to Gen AI: The Impact and Opportunities and Challenges of Gen AI for Young Australians. In a recent episode of the AI in Education Podcast (2025), Denejkina reminded us that the best way to understand AI in schools is not to theorise what young people should be doing, but to pay attention to what they are doing.

"This series is all about students," she explained. "It's what students are doing, not what they should do, not what anybody else thinks they're doing—and the research that came out just gives that fantastic insight." (AI in Education Podcast, 15 August 2025).

Her point is simple but profound: the student voice must sit at the centre of how we respond to AI in education. Without it, we risk creating policies, lessons, and tools that miss the mark.

What Students Are Really Doing with AI

The narrative in the media often paints young people as either passive consumers or crafty cheaters when it comes to AI. But Denejkina's findings—and the stories many of us see daily in classrooms—tell a different story.

Students are:

- Using AI for brainstorming ideas when they're stuck.
- Seeking clarity on concepts they didn't fully grasp in class.
- Experimenting with rewriting, simplifying, or extending their work.
- Playing with creativity — writing poems, making images, or simulating scenarios.

This is not about laziness. It is about exploration. For Gen Z, AI is not a "special tool" — it is a natural extension of the digital ecosystems they already inhabit. Just as calculators and Google searches became embedded into study habits, so too will AI.

And yet, they are also deeply uncertain. Many aren't sure where the ethical lines are. They wonder, "Is this allowed?" "Does this count as plagiarism?" "What if I rely on it too much?"

This tension between capability and uncertainty is where adults must step in — not to police, but to guide.

The Paradox of Capability and Uncertainty

One of the most striking aspects of Denejkina's research is the gap between what students can do with AI and what they feel confident doing.

On the one hand, they are digital natives who can navigate layered, interactive environments like gaming, where complex decision-making and resilience are second nature. On the other hand, many lack the prompting literacy or critical frameworks to use AI effectively in academic contexts.

I've seen this in my own home. My son once attempted to use AI for a Physical Education assessment task (in which AI was approved in Part A only), only to get stuck at the very first hurdle: how to phrase a useful prompt. He had the vision—he wanted to build a self-reflection survey—but didn't yet have the academic fluency to draw it out of the AI.

This is exactly where Michael McDowell's Surface–Deep–Transfer model of learning becomes critical. At first, students need guidance at the surface level—

learning the mechanics of prompting and experimenting with tools. With feedback and support, they move into deep learning, where they question, refine, and evaluate AI outputs. Ultimately, the goal is transfer — applying those skills across subjects, tasks, and real-world contexts.

Without this scaffolding, uncertainty becomes paralysis. With it, AI becomes empowerment.

Student Anxieties and Aspirations

Denejkina's research also shines a light on the emotional landscape of Gen Z in the AI era. Students are not only using AI to learn — they are wrestling with how it fits into their identity and aspirations.

For some, AI is a safety net. It reduces stress by offering a starting point when the blank page feels overwhelming. For others, it raises anxiety: "If AI can do this better than me, what's the point of trying?"

This duality matters. As parents and educators, we need to affirm that AI is not here to replace effort, but to amplify it. One student captured this perfectly when she reflected, "I didn't think you would notice if I just got AI to do it. But when you showed me how to use Gemini, I realised that I could work with it and that made me happy because I actually want to do my own work."

That insight is gold. It points us to a future where AI becomes less of a crutch and more of a coach.

Implications for Parents

For parents, the message is clear: don't bury your head in the sand. Ask your children what they're doing with AI. Invite them to show you how they're using it. Create space for conversations about not just what they can do, but what they should do.

Questions like:

- "How did AI help you today?"
- "Do you agree with the answer it gave? Why or why not?"
- "How are you going to fact check that information?"

- "What do you think the limits of AI should be?"

These conversations don't just build digital literacy. They build ethical literacy.

Implications for Teachers

Teachers, too, cannot afford avoidance. As Denejkina's research highlights, students are already using these tools. The real question is whether they are using them well.

The role of the teacher is not diminished — it is redefined. Teachers remain the anchors of values, discernment, and human connection. AI may answer 1,500 student questions in a night (as one economics teacher found), but it cannot look a student in the eye, notice their anxiety, or celebrate their growth. Students still want that.

The opportunity for teachers is to model AI use, scaffold prompting, and co-design learning tasks that blend human creativity with machine support. As Lyn Sharratt's work reveals, the power of pedagogy lies in precision: knowing what each learner needs, and responding with clarity and care. AI gives us tools to extend this precision—but pedagogy must lead the technology, not the other way around.

Neuroscience: Why Student Voice Matters

Understanding why student voice matters requires looking at what happens inside your child's developing brain. When children have genuine choices in their learning, three crucial neurological processes occur that shape their lifelong capacity for growth and success.

First, student choice activates the brain's reward system. When your child chooses what or how to learn, their brain releases dopamine - the same chemical that creates feelings of satisfaction and accomplishment. This generates intrinsic motivation that sustains engagement far beyond external rewards like stickers or grades, making learning feel naturally rewarding rather than burdensome.

Second, self-directed learning strengthens the prefrontal cortex - essentially your child's brain "CEO" that handles planning, working memory, and flexible thinking.

Children literally build the neural pathways they'll need for problem-solving, organisation, and adapting to new situations throughout their lives. It's cognitive fitness training for lifelong learning.

Finally, having autonomy reduces cortisol production, eliminating stress hormones that impair memory formation. Simultaneously, active engagement enhances the hippocampus - the brain's memory centre - making it easier for children to retain and apply what they've learnt.

Your child's brain is constantly reshaping itself based on experiences. When children feel silenced or powerless, stress circuits dominate, interfering with both learning and wellbeing. However, when they're invited to question, reflect, and contribute meaningfully to their education,

neuroplasticity strengthens. They literally rewire their brains for confidence, resilience, and independent thinking through the simple act of being heard and valued.

That is why Denejkina's insistence on listening to what students are doing is not just good research—it's good neuroscience.

Final Thought: Listening as Leadership

The voices of Gen Z are not background noise in the AI revolution—they are the signal, the compass pointing toward the future of learning. They show us how they are already navigating the opportunities and pitfalls of AI, blending curiosity with caution, creativity with critical thinking. To ignore them is to risk creating schools, policies, and practices that fall short. To truly listen is to craft systems that amplify their strengths, support their struggles, and prepare them not merely to survive, but to thrive in a rapidly evolving world. As Dr. Anna Denejkina's research invites us to consider that, the story of AI in education is not about machines—it is about students, their experiences, and the ways they shape knowledge every day. Our greatest responsibility, then, is not to control, but to listen, guide, and believe them when they say, 'This is how we learn now, and this is how we will change tomorrow.'

CHAPTER 10:
THE POWER OF PLAY AND CREATIVITY

Not long after leaving school, I saw what was possible when my son was free to be himself. On a rainy afternoon, still raw from a breakup, he dusted off his guitar. Within minutes, the lounge room was filled with music — aching, searching, healing. He had found a way to express what words could not, a way to express emotions that had been bottled up.

Music became his therapy, and soon, his identity. He and his mates formed a band — the Bakers Green — and began rehearsing in our garage. They were protective of their sound, often waiting until we were out before practising, so we only ever heard fragments. Neighbours would occasionally mention, "They're good," but we had no idea what to expect.

Their first real test came with a gig at a local venue. The condition was clear: they had to perform two original songs. My son helped write both. Family and friends travelled from out of town. As parents, we were nervous — proud, but anxious. Could they really pull this off?

When the lead singer's first note wavered, my heart dropped. But then — something clicked. They found their rhythm and my family all looked at each other and smiled knowing smiles, the room came alive. My son was glowing, completely in his element. At that moment, surrounded by people who loved him, I realised he hadn't just found a hobby — he had found a home for his heart.

Though my son eventually moved in a different direction, some of those original friends carried the dream forward. They evolved into the band Korderoy, who now have albums and music streaming on Spotify. It's a proud reminder of how small beginnings in a garage can grow into something extraordinary.

That night taught me something profound. Creativity isn't just an outlet; it's a lifeline. It heals, motivates, and helps young people take ownership of their own growth. And whether it leads to a career, a passion project, or simply a way to process life, the act of creating itself is transformative.

For Darren and I, it was also a turning point in our parenting. We had always valued academic success — grades, discipline, measurable outcomes. But watching our son transform through music forced us to ask a harder question: what if the most important education doesn't come from textbooks at all? What if creativity is not a luxury, but a necessity?

When we give our children permission to create — whether through music, sport, storytelling, or play — we give them tools that no algorithm can replicate: resilience, self-expression, and the courage to be themselves.

That experience reshaped how we parented and how we taught. It cemented for us the absolute need to nurture creativity alongside academics, not as an optional extra, but as a foundation for resilience, self-expression, and the courage to be themselves. And in an age of AI — where algorithms can memorise, calculate, and even compose — the human act of creating remains one of the greatest gifts we can protect in our children.

Neuroscience Drop-in: Darren Gray

Creative learning activates multiple brain networks simultaneously, creating optimal conditions for knowledge acquisition and retention. When students engage in creative activities, the default mode network — including the medial prefrontal cortex — generates novel ideas through divergent thinking, while the executive attention network evaluates and refines these concepts.

The brain switches between focused attention and diffuse thinking modes during creative learning. This alternation allows for both concentrated study and the wandering mind states where breakthrough insights often occur. Educational environments incorporating both structured instruction and open exploration harness this natural rhythm effectively.

The hippocampus plays a crucial role by connecting disparate information in novel ways. Creative activities encourage the formation of new neural pathways between previously unconnected concepts, thereby strengthening overall comprehension and promoting neuroplasticity – the brain's ability to reorganise and form new connections.

Creative learning activates the brain's reward system through the release of dopamine during "aha!" moments, creating positive associations with education and enhancing motivation. This neurochemical response consolidates learning by strengthening memory traces.

Unlike traditional approaches that emphasise left-brain analytical thinking, creative learning engages both hemispheres simultaneously. This bilateral activation promotes enhanced cross-hemispheric communication, developing more robust and flexible thinking patterns essential for innovative problem-solving and academic success across multiple domains.

AI Can Support, Not Replace, Creative Thought

Used thoughtfully, AI can also spark creativity. In my Japanese classroom, I've seen students light up as they use AI tools like Gemini or Copilot to co-write travel brochures or invent imaginary towns. One student put it simply: "It's like having someone who helps me... but never makes me feel dumb."

We prompt each other on the board: "Help me write three sentences about a town festival in Kobe," or "Suggest a Japanese food for a Year 7 student to describe." Each student works at their level, at their own pace — scaffolded by me and supported by AI. It's not a shortcut; it's a launchpad. They still have to think, translate, create. But they're not stuck. And when they get to the end of the task, there's pride. They've made something real. Their confidence builds not from praise, but from seeing what they can do.

We can't cling to order and uniformity, then hope for innovation. Creativity needs space — and so do our children

The Neuroscience of Play and Imagination

Play isn't just downtime—it's brain work. Dr Stuart Brown, founder of the National Institute for Play, describes play as "the gateway to vitality." Through play, children develop essential skills, including executive function, emotional regulation, and problem-solving. Activities like pretend play and improvisational games activate the

brain's prefrontal cortex, which is key to decision-making and planning.

Darren explains it this way, "When children play freely, their brains form flexible pathways for adaptive thinking. These neural circuits lay the foundation for creativity, resilience, and innovation later in life."

Unstructured play helps consolidate learning, reduce stress, and improve emotional regulation. Creative activities, such as music, drawing, or storytelling, increase dopamine (which boosts motivation) and reduce cortisol (which lowers stress).

Practical Tips for Parents: Nurturing Creativity and Play at Home

1. Provide Open-Ended Materials

Offer tools that don't come with instructions, such as cardboard boxes, LEGOs, musical instruments, markers, and costume pieces. Let them invent.

2. Honour Creative Time

Block out time in the week for creative exploration — where the goal isn't productivity, but play. No outcomes. No assessments.

3. Embrace Mistakes

Show that creativity involves trial and error. Share your projects or hobbies that didn't go as planned — and what you learned.

4. Use AI as a Creative Partner

Explore AI together: prompt it to generate the first line of a story, or suggest song lyrics. Then let your child take it from there. The key is not replacing their imagination, but fuelling it.

5. Ask Process-Based Questions

Rather than "What did you make?", ask "What did you enjoy most?" or "What surprised you?" This shifts the focus from product to process.

6. Model Playfulness

Join in! Build a fort, write a silly poem, paint with your fingers. Your participation signals that creativity is valued.

Reflection Prompts for Families

- When do your children seem most creative?
- How do you respond when they show you their creations?
- What space (physical or emotional) do you provide for imagination at home?

- How might you model creativity in your own life?

Final Thought

Creativity is not just a phase of childhood. It's the spark of innovation, the tool of emotional resilience, and the root of human connection. It enables children to process emotions, explore new ideas, and imagine possibilities beyond the present confines. Whether it's through strumming a guitar after heartbreak, scribbling a poem in a quiet notebook, or exploring an AI-generated idea that ignites curiosity, creativity gives children the means to make sense of their world—and to find their place within it.

As parents and educators, we are not just raising students. We are nurturing storytellers, designers, builders, and dreamers. We have the opportunity—and responsibility—to provide them with permission, encouragement, and the space to experiment, fail, and try again. When we do, we are not only fostering innovation; we are cultivating empathy, confidence, and the courage to create a life that is uniquely their own. Let us champion creativity, not as a luxury, but as an essential foundation for growth, learning, and human flourishing.

CHAPTER 11: RAISING INDEPENDENT LEARNERS

Not long ago, I watched my eldest son — who had once been so lost and anxious — step onto a plane bound for Japan. It was his first solo trip overseas. My husband and I thought we had prepared for every possibility: spreadsheets, shared digital itineraries, emergency contacts and transport guides. We had covered every detail — or so we believed.

A last-minute change in accommodation meant that, at 2 a.m. in Shibuya, Japan he and his friend arrived at the wrong hotel, towing suitcases and a snowboard bag. He didn't call. He figured it out. Later, he navigated rural Japan, sorted out meals, and even hired a car to explore other areas, something we determinedly didn't help him with as we didn't want him driving in the snow! That trip became the ultimate symbol of independence — not because everything went smoothly, but because when it didn't, he handled it.

This journey, like his choice to pursue music over more conventional paths, reminded me of a powerful truth: independence is not born from control. It is forged in trust.

Our younger son, by contrast, is a self-directed and passionate learner, with a razor-sharp focus on his goals. He is a dedicated basketball referee and sets high standards for himself. Unlike his brother, who thrives creatively, our younger son thrives in structure and purpose. He holds himself accountable and uses technology in different but equally powerful ways. He spends time analysing game footage, upskilling through referee training videos, and following elite-level officiating conversations on social media. He connects with peers and mentors, builds his network, and is actively growing his knowledge base in the world he cares about most.

Recently, for an assessment that he asked me to look over, I explained to him that the days of simply dropping facts onto a PowerPoint are long gone. In today's digital landscape, young people need to create engaging content that effectively conveys their message. We discussed how modern athletes—especially those competing at the Olympics—must now understand the importance of branding and content creation. It's not enough to win races. Sponsors want personalities with a following on social media. We have a friend who's a professional triathlete and despite his remarkable performance, he has been fortunate that his sponsors have remained loyal. His time is far better spent training than creating content but the rise of influencers has changed the game.

Not long after this assessment task by younger son he decided to apply for his first job—at a major national sports clothing retail store. I explained to him that it would be very rare for someone at a company like this to actually read a resume. Instead it would be scanned by AI for keywords. Instead of asking me to help write his resume, he turned to AI. He started by asking Gemini:

"What qualities do Rebel Sport look for in an employee?"

Then he searched for the keywords and action phrases that employers scan for in resumes. Using that, he uploaded his experiences—his basketball refereeing, volunteer coaching, sports carnivals—and asked the AI to match his skills to the job description. It helped him write compelling dot points that actually aligned with the language used by the company.

Then, with a level of maturity I hadn't expected, he asked:

"What's missing from my application? What else do I need to add? What could make me not get the job?"

The AI offered suggestions—not just about skills but soft factors like availability, customer interaction, and teamwork examples. He adjusted his resume accordingly. It wasn't just a form—it became a strategic document, tailored and personalised.

This wasn't about cheating. It was about empowerment.

Despite applying online, he still walked into the store and delivered his resume with confidence because he knew that his resume aligned with their company's HR hiring policy. I didn't have the heart to tell him that they only hire from 16 years and above. To me it was a great learning opportunity. AI helped him prepare. It helped him understand what employers value, how to articulate his strengths, and how to fill in the gaps.

This is what we mean when we talk about raising future-ready learners. It's not just about tech savviness— it's about self-awareness, initiative, and agency. My son didn't wait for someone else to do it for him. He used the tools available to step into his future with clarity, purpose and confidence.

Why Independent Learning Matters More Than Ever

In an AI-driven world, where automation handles increasingly complex tasks, human value lies in decision-making, initiative, and adaptability. Independent learners don't wait for instructions—they anticipate, explore, and problem-solve. They aren't afraid to fail, because they view failure as a natural part of the process.

Neuroscience supports this. In our own conversations about learning and the brain, Darren points out that, "the prefrontal cortex — the part of the brain responsible for planning, self-regulation, and initiative — strengthens through repeated practice. When children make choices and solve problems independently, they build the neural architecture required for real-world resilience."

Yet, fostering independence can feel counterintuitive. We want to help. We want to prevent struggle. But often, it's in the battle that learning takes root.

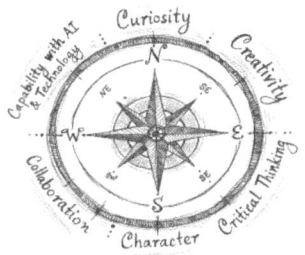

The Classroom: Independence in Action

Teaching a topic based on the History of the Catholic Church in Australia in Year 9 Religion is not, by any stretch, what most students would consider thrilling. It's often met with glazed eyes and half-hearted paragraphs. I've taught it enough times to know which sections feel inaccessible—and this time, I was prepared to take the pressure off. As it wasn't a formally assessed area, I told students they could submit whatever they had finished. No stress.

But then something unexpected happened. At the end of the lesson, a handful of students stopped me.

"Miss… do we have to hand it in today?"

"Can I keep working on it over the weekend and hand it in on Tuesday?"

I was stunned. Not because the work wasn't worthy of extra time — but because they genuinely wanted more time. They weren't asking for an extension out of panic or procrastination. They weren't done… because they weren't done exploring.

The task was simple in theory: design a new parish for our local area, including a community outreach program tailored to the needs of that community. Students used AI tools like Gemini and Copilot to research local demographics. Previously, they would have relied on the 2021 National Census data — accurate, yes, but now four years old. With AI, they accessed more current, nuanced insights into housing stress, unemployment, cultural diversity, and access to services.

They began asking thoughtful questions:

- Who lives here?
- What challenges do they face?
- What kind of support would make a difference?

And then they started designing—not just buildings, but purpose-built spaces with meaning.

They used platforms like Roblox, Minecraft, and Sims—usually seen as play—but now transformed into design studios. Many of these tools weren't fully accessible at school, so students asked to continue their projects at home. Not because they had to—because they wanted to.

One student with known learning differences was waiting at the door Tuesday morning, grinning from ear to ear.

"Miss! I finished it! Can I show you?"

She gave me a full walkthrough of her digital parish—complete with inclusive ramps, a multi-faith prayer room, a pop-up café that doubled as a food bank, and a community garden to support mental and physical well-being. She had embedded empathy into every design choice.

Another student was knocking on the door early, eager to show off his project. He was proud—really proud. And it wasn't about the mark. He was proud of his work. Another girl who rarely engages in any conversation with me got out of her chair to show me and I could see the pride. I asked, 'Would you go to this church?' She replied with. 'Miss, this is the type of church I would get married in'.

This is what happens when technology meets agency.

- When students aren't forced to engage—they choose to.
- When creativity isn't boxed in by worksheets—but expanded by tools they already know and love.
- When assessment becomes authentic, empowering, and deeply personal.

These weren't just digital projects. They were reflections of how students see the world—and how they want to improve it. This wasn't compliance. It was a connection.

So often in classrooms, I notice students disengage unless something is being marked. "Is this for assessment?" is the most common question. It's as if learning only matters if it counts towards a report. But this project proved otherwise. They weren't motivated by marks—they were motivated by meaning.

And that's what the future of education must lean into:

Purpose-driven learning. Real-world relevance. Student ownership. That's when you know learning is alive—and that's independence.

What the Research Says

Contrary to fears that AI makes students lazy or dishonest, recent research paints a different picture. A 2023 report from the Stanford Graduate School of Education found that most students use AI not to cheat, but to learn—especially when they are given clear guidance and ethical frameworks.

We've seen this before with technology. Phones, once seen as distractions, are now where we bank, shop, follow recipes, navigate, research, connect and create. In many ways, they have already levelled the playing field—placing tools into every hand that once depended on privilege, older siblings, or tutors. AI is simply the next extension of this shift.

But having access is not the same as mastery. Many adults feel left behind by technology, and yet students, too, often only know how to use devices within narrow habits. This is where our role as parents and educators comes in—not simply allowing AI, but teaching young people to use it wisely, ethically, and to the best of their capability.

I was proud when my younger son once said to me, "Mum, I need to learn how to do this myself. I need to learn how to summarise and take notes from AI. That's an important skill too." He was right. That kind of self-awareness — choosing discernment over dependency — is exactly what we want for our kids.

Initially, when he began experimenting with AI, he quickly discovered it wasn't as simple as typing a question and using AI the same as a google search. A recent Year 9 commerce assessment provided the perfect testing ground. The task required students to create a marketing campaign for a new product. Part A allowed the use of AI for research and development, while Part B was a live presentation and reflection to demonstrate independent understanding.

He had a brilliant concept for a sustainable streetwear brand — but no idea how to begin developing a targeted marketing strategy. Together, we reviewed his ideas, then used Gemini to help structure a promotional pitch. He asked it to identify key demographic segments, suggest persuasive slogans, and even evaluate the social media platforms most likely to reach Gen Z consumers. From there, he adapted the content, created a campaign slide deck, and integrated the materials into his Google

Site. His final pitch was engaging and cohesive—but most importantly, it was his.

What stood out to me throughout the process was his growing awareness of how to prompt well. In earlier attempts, he'd asked vague questions and received generic answers. Now, he was learning to refine his language: "Generate five slogans that teenagers would immediately relate to," or "Compare TikTok and Instagram for reach among 13-17-year-olds." He wasn't just using AI—he was guiding it with intention.

This is exactly what Michael McDowell refers to in his Surface-Deep-Transfer model. At the surface level, students need help understanding the tool—how it works, how to ask questions, and how to interpret responses. With guided practice, they move to deep learning, refining outputs, asking better questions, and using AI to complement their thinking rather than replace it. Ultimately, they reach the transfer phase, where they can use these skills in new contexts—across subjects, tasks, and even life beyond school.

In this task, my son didn't just learn about marketing. He learned how to learn with AI. This is why prompting is not just a digital skill — it's a new form of literacy. We can't assume students will know how to do this instinctively. Just like we teach paragraph structure or mathematical reasoning, we must also explicitly teach ethical prompting, iterative questioning, and critical analysis of outputs.

AI, like the calculator or smartphone before it, puts creativity, problem-solving, and knowledge generation within reach for all learners. But unless students are shown how to move from basic use, to intentional application, to transferable insight, its promise will remain unevenly distributed.

We must teach students how to wield these tools — not just to complete tasks, but to express ideas, solve problems, and navigate complexity. When we do, we are not just improving their academic fluency. We are preparing them for a world where the ability to think with AI will define not just success, but contribution.

Darren's Neuroscience Drop-In: Brain Rot or Brain Growth?

Headlines about AI and the brain can be dramatic. In August 2025, The Diary of a CEO podcast ran with the title: *"ChatGPT Brain Rot: The Fastest Way to Get Dementia."* It drew on an MIT study claiming a 47% drop in brain activity and poorer memory scores when people used ChatGPT to write compared with writing unaided. It's the kind of headline that sends shockwaves through homes and classrooms. And, as a neuroscientist, I want to call it what it is: ***a scare tactic.***

Parents and schools could easily respond with a knee-jerk reaction—ban AI, shut it down, and pretend it isn't part of our children's future. But history tells us that this approach backfires. We saw it with calculators, the internet, even smartphones. Early adopters who learned to use these tools critically and creatively ended up with the advantage, while those who avoided them had to catch up later.

It's also important to keep some perspective. There are many things that we know can damage the brain and increase the risk of dementia: excessive alcohol, nicotine, head trauma, untreated high blood pressure, sleep deprivation, chronic stress, and even some artificial sweeteners that have been linked to impaired brain health. These are lifestyle factors with far stronger evidence of long-term harm than responsible use of AI. The difference is, we don't ban cars because people crash them, or outlaw sugar because it can cause disease. Instead, we set guardrails, encourage moderation, and teach safe, informed habits. AI deserves the same approach.

Dr Daniel Amen's brain imaging research reveals to us that the brain is remarkably resilient. With the right habits—nutrition, exercise, restorative sleep, and meaningful mental challenge—it can grow stronger, even after setbacks.

Passive AI use – simply copying outputs or outsourcing thought – does risk under-activating the prefrontal cortex, the area responsible for planning and focus. Over time, unused pathways weaken. But active use – questioning, comparing, iterating, and creating – stimulates neuroplasticity, strengthens memory, and builds the higher-order skills our children will need to thrive.

So, will ChatGPT cause "brain rot"? No. The real danger is letting fear drive us into avoidance. Banning AI in schools or homes doesn't protect students – it deprives them of the chance to practise using it well. Early adopters who embrace it with curiosity, guardrails, and guidance will benefit most, developing the very skills that machines cannot replicate: critical thinking, creativity, ethics, empathy, and adaptability.

Parents and educators don't need to fear AI. What we need is the courage to guide children in using it wisely — because the future won't belong to those who avoid these tools, but to those who learn how to use them with intention.

Practical Tips for Parents

1. Build Gradual Responsibility

Let your child plan part of a trip, choose a project topic, or manage a family task. Independence builds through doing.

2. Embrace Mistakes as Milestones

When your child stumbles — forgetting homework, booking the wrong accommodation, misusing a tool — help them reflect and learn. Don't solve it. Please support them in solving it.

3. Teach Prompting Skills

Practice writing prompts together. Show them how to iterate. Try: "Rewrite this paragraph for Year 7 students," or "Give me three alternatives for this sentence." Let them see the power of intelligent prompting.

4. Scaffold, Then Step Back

Be present early in a task, then gradually remove support. Please encourage them to work through confusion rather than rescuing them at the first sign of struggle.

5. Model Independence Yourself

Share your own planning processes — how you organise your day, troubleshoot at work, or manage finances. Let them see that independence is a journey, not an instant switch.

Reflection Prompts for Families

- In what areas is your child already independent?
- Where do they tend to seek help quickly — and how can you support them to think first?
- What does independence look like in your family? How is it nurtured?

Final Thought

We often confuse independence with solitude. But true freedom is about agency — knowing that you have tools, support, and confidence to face challenges. Whether it's navigating Tokyo at 2 a.m., researching a town in Japanese, translating scripture into Gen Z or Gen Alpha metaphors, building a personal brand as a referee, or designing a parish crest that responds to modern needs, our children are capable of more than we imagine.

What they need isn't us doing it for them. They need us beside them — believing they can.

That's how independent learners are made.

Let's trust them enough to let them try.

CHAPTER 12:
THE ART OF LETTING GO

One of the most pervasive parenting assumptions is that we understand youth because we were once young ourselves. But today's children are not growing up in a slightly modified version of our world — they're navigating an entirely different landscape, shaped by the forces of rapid technological change, relentless digital stimulation, and mounting social pressure. The gap between generations has never been more profound.

When I give students my yearly "learning preferences" questionnaire, I've noticed a striking trend: an overwhelming number of students say their least favourite activity is speaking in front of the class. Of course, public speaking has always made some people nervous. But this is different. This represents a generation-wide withdrawal from being seen and heard in real-time. I can ask a question to the whole class, knowing that more than half of the students know the answer, and still be met with silence. It's not laziness or lack of knowledge—it's fear.

The Silent Classroom

This shift is supported by current research. A study published in the Journal of Educational Psychology (2022) found that more than 70% of high school students experience moderate to severe anxiety related to in-class verbal participation. A 2023 report by ReachOut Australia revealed a marked increase in classroom communication anxiety, particularly in secondary schools, with students citing fear of judgment, canceled culture, and comparison exacerbated by social media as key contributors. Many feel more comfortable submitting work digitally than speaking aloud, even in small groups.

The rise of a performative culture—where every utterance can be recorded, shared, or judged—has cultivated a generation that is more comfortable typing than talking. However, this matters because oral communication remains one of the most crucial human skills we can develop in young people.

We must rethink how we teach students to speak, to share, and to be seen—not as perfect orators, but as people with something to say. And as parents, we must let go of the belief that we already know what it means to be a young person today. We don't. But we can learn.

What We Don't See: Learning from the Unspoken Digital Rules of Youth

Recently, I attended a wedding (of an ex-student)—my first in a while. While there were traditional paper invitations, most of the details were shared online, and I'll admit, I missed a few. I was the only one who brought a physical gift, not realising that the couple had moved to digital gifting and group contributions. Later, I wanted to post a photo of us together but I paused (thankfully). Don't post before the bride!! Golden Rule.

That hesitation wasn't random. It was digital etiquette. And it made me realise: young people live by these unspoken rules every day. Their world is governed by an emotional grammar — non-verbal, nuanced, and constantly evolving — yet often invisible to adults.

We assume they're addicted to their screens, disconnected from real relationships. But what if we've been looking at it all wrong?

In the Netflix documentary Adolescence, teens speak about their online lives with raw honesty. They know when someone's ignoring them. They notice who watches their stories but never interacts. They feel the chill of being "left on read," and they understand when someone is signalling support — or silently withdrawing it. I learnt that the colour of emoji speaks volumes.

This is a sophisticated emotional landscape, full of rituals and etiquette that we, as adults, often dismiss, ridicule or overlook.

Why This Matters

Adults often dismiss online behaviour as superficial. We say, "It's just social media," or "They're obsessed with streaks and likes." But these platforms are today's primary social arenas. Just as we learned how to read body language, navigate a phone call, or shake hands appropriately — this generation has learned how to read the digital room. Most of this is undetected by parents.

What looks like scrolling may actually be social maintenance. What appears like silence may actually be coded support. And what we see as obsession with followers might actually be about belonging, affirmation, and emotional safety.

Psychologist Sherry Turkle argues that teens today "are not antisocial — they're differently social." Their digital identities are layered and performative, but also incredibly vulnerable.

Educators and parents need to understand that digital citizenship isn't just about safety. It's about empathy, identity, boundaries, and community. When a teen doesn't post for weeks, that could mean more than "they're busy." When someone deletes a post after an hour, it might not have gotten "enough" likes. Or maybe it attracted the wrong kind of attention. These actions carry weight. From a business perspective if you are trying to build a digital presence you simply can not 'post and ghost'. It is essential to engage with your followers and audience. Every single business owner now must be a marketing guru. Employees that know this skill will be invaluable.

What We Can Learn

Rather than rolling our eyes at online culture, we have an opportunity to listen, observe, and ask. Teenagers aren't just the users of digital tools — they're often the innovators of unspoken digital language.

And when we approach with curiosity, not judgement, we learn that:

- Their rules are based on respect (don't post before the bride, ask before tagging).
- Their rituals are grounded in empathy (replying with speed, noticing who's silent).
- Their platforms are spaces of performance — but also places of truth.

Instead of asking "Why are you always online?", we can ask:

- "How do you show support to your friends digitally?"
- "What do you notice when someone stops engaging?"
- "What does a 'comment' mean to you compared to a 'like'?"

These questions open doors — not just to understanding their world, but to becoming trusted allies in it.

In a time when young people are often painted as disconnected, this insight flips the script. They are deeply connected — but by rules we don't always see.

Maybe it's time we started learning from them, too.

Boys and the Future of Leadership

Recently at our school, something subtle — but significant — happened. It was time for student leadership nominations, particularly for the prestigious House Captain roles. Traditionally, each house elects one male and one female leader. But this year, we didn't have enough boys step forward to nominate themselves—or be nominated by their peers.

In the end, each house appointed two female leaders. This wasn't due to a lack of capable boys. It was because they didn't want to put themselves forward.

This pattern isn't isolated to our school. Across many educational contexts, we're seeing a similar trend: boys showing increasing reluctance to place themselves "above" their peers. But that doesn't mean they don't want to lead. It means they are reimagining leadership.

There's a shift in peer culture where leadership is no longer about hierarchy, visibility, or dominance. For many boys, putting your hand up to lead can be perceived as a sign of self-importance or superiority—qualities that clash with a deepening cultural emphasis on sameness and peer-level equality. Instead, boys are gravitating toward leadership that is collaborative, horizontal, and embedded in teamwork.

This mindset parallels the culture of online multiplayer gaming — an environment many boys navigate daily. In these games, success isn't about individual heroism, but about coordinated effort. Roles are fluid, everyone contributes, and leadership emerges from trust, not titles. Boys are bringing that ethos into real life.

A 2020 report by the Australian Council for Educational Research highlighted shifting student leadership patterns, noting that boys are increasingly opting for quiet leadership roles or working collaboratively rather than seeking traditional, performative positions. Similarly, social psychologist Dr Niobe Way has explored how boys, particularly in late adolescence, often prioritise relationships and equality over dominance, especially when peer expectations discourage standing out.

They're not disengaged — they're communicating something powerful, albeit silently: leadership, for them, is about being embedded in the team, not elevated above it.

As educators and parents, we must expand our definition of leadership. Leadership can look like initiating a group project idea, mentoring a younger student, moderating a team in an online community, or offering emotional support behind the scenes. These are all forms of leadership that today's boys value.

To nurture this, we should:

- Recognise and celebrate collaborative and relational leadership styles.
- Provide team-based leadership opportunities where students co-lead rather than compete.
- Normalise leadership as service, contribution, and shared responsibility.

In a world increasingly shaped by connection and co-creation, our boys may be leading us toward a better model—one grounded in humility, teamwork, and mutual respect. And we would be wise to listen.

Letting Go of the Illusion of Sameness

Letting go isn't only about expectations—it's also about assumptions. Many parents assume their children's school struggles or anxieties mirror their own teen experiences. But the challenges facing young people today are entirely new. Mental health is declining, digital identity is overwhelming, and the pressure to always be "on" is relentless.

Instead of assuming we understand, we must become listeners. We must get curious. Ask questions. Hold back our solutions and be brave enough to let our kids teach us what it's like to grow up now.

You Never Know Who You're Teaching

There's something strange and wonderful about standing in a classroom, looking out over a group of students, and realising—you have no idea who they're going to become. You hope you're equipping them with something meaningful. But the truth is, at the moment, you're mostly just trying to get through the lesson plan, reach the student in the back row, and survive bus duty.

Our school has seen its fair share of well-known names pass through the halls over the years. Take Baz Luhrmann, for example. The filmmaker behind Moulin Rouge, The Great Gatsby, and Elvis once walked the halls of our original campus. Someone whose stories now reach the world once sat in the same classrooms, tripped through the same hallways, and probably posed for the same awkward school photos as everyone else. I like to imagine he was already dreaming big back then—even if it was just doodling ideas in a notebook during lessons.

Then there's James Magnussen. The London 2012 Olympic silver medallist and a former world champion in the swimming 100m freestyle. Even as a student, James had this quiet intensity. You could tell he was different—confident, driven, the kind of kid who wasn't afraid to push himself. Honestly, it didn't surprise anyone when he went on to make waves on the international stage.

And Riley Batt… now Riley's story is something special. I first met him in Year 6 when I was teaching at a primary school. Our parish schools went on a combined camp, and Riley made an impression straight away. He wasn't in a wheelchair back then—he zipped around on a skateboard, fast, fearless, and always grinning. I can't remember a single time when Riley wasn't smiling. Cheeky, full of energy, totally unfazed by the world around him.

A few years later, I ended up teaching Riley — this time in high school, as his PE teacher. And, well... he was using a wheelchair now, and I had no idea what I was doing. The class was tough—26 energetic kids, most needing constant attention. Riley? He was more capable than I could fully grasp. But I hadn't had any training, and my 'best' never seemed enough.

I remember this one lesson vividly. Riley had wheeled himself down to the oval and was just... sitting there. He must have been so bored. I kept looking over at him and felt that guilty hit again. I didn't know how to include him. A football in his hand? Totally didn't even think of it.

We laugh about that now. I still keep in touch with Riley, and I tell him honestly: I probably learned more from him than he ever did from me. The things he went on to achieve—representing Australia, multiple Paralympic golds, a paralympian Australian flag bearer, fearless leader and advocate—well, it still leaves me speechless.

There's a lesson in this. Maybe several. About resilience, about perspective, and about how much we can learn when we stop worrying about doing everything "right" and start paying attention to the people in front of us. We don't always know how to meet every student's needs. We don't always know what they're capable of. But that's never an excuse to stop trying. We must keep finding other ways.

For Riley, a football in his hand would've changed everything in that moment. And in a way, it eventually did.

This story has stayed with me throughout my career. It reminded me that the child you don't quite know how to teach today might become the person you're proudest to know tomorrow. And that every single student deserves the chance to find their thing—the tool, the subject, the moment—that unlocks their potential.

Whether it's an AI prompt, a skateboard, a microphone, or a swimming lane—every child has something that will set them free.

As educators and parents, our job isn't to have all the answers. It's to look again. To ask differently. To offer the football, even if we're not sure how they'll use it. Because you never know who you're teaching.

New Skills for a New World

If the world has changed, so must our definition of success. We must raise children who are:

- Empathetic – able to connect, listen, and navigate complex relationships, both online and off.
- Curious – eager to explore ideas without the fear of "getting it wrong."
- Creative – capable of building, designing, composing, and expressing.

- Critical Thinkers – able to question, analyse, and challenge misinformation.
- Effective Communicators – confident in speaking, writing, and visual storytelling.
- Digitally Literate – aware of how their online presence shapes opportunities and perceptions.

From Control to Curiosity

Letting go of control was the hardest lesson of all. For so long, I believed my role was to keep our children on the "right" path. But when my eldest asked me quietly, "Can I, Mum?" — seeking permission to follow his passion — it struck me that my job was not to dictate the path, but to walk beside him as he carved his own.

Today, he is thriving in a Bachelor of Sound Engineering at SAE, motivated, focused, and alive with purpose. What once felt like failure has become freedom — for both of us. And the lesson hasn't been his alone. Our younger son is still in school, but his strengths are different. He is developing as a basketball referee, analysing plays online, setting high standards for himself, and building a name in his field. His path looks nothing like his brother's, but it carries the same truth: identity is not forged by ticking academic boxes. It is found in following what lights you up.

This journey has shifted me as a parent. I no longer ask, "How do I keep them on track?" Instead, I ask, "What makes them come alive—and how can I support it?" Letting go of control and stepping into curiosity has changed everything.

Practical Tips for Parents

1. Reimagine Communication

Offer low-stakes opportunities to practise speaking, such as dinner conversations, audio messages, family presentations, or even TikToks explaining a topic of interest.

2. Model Digital Confidence

Discuss your learning curve with technology. Show your child how you make sense of misinformation or construct an ethical online presence.

3. Create Safe Speaking Spaces

Don't always correct. Sometimes, just hearing themselves speak without interruption can build trust.

4. Honour Different Paths

University isn't the only avenue. Passion-led careers, microcredentials, apprenticeships, and creator-based work are all valid.

5. Accept Change as Growth

Their dreams may change. That's okay. Our job is to evolve with them, not hold them to the version we once imagined.

Reflection Questions

- Where might I be assuming I already understand what my child is going through?
- What new skill, rather than old advice, could I help them develop?
- Have I confused 'support' with 'control'? What might letting go look like?

Final Thought

Letting go as a parent isn't giving up — it's giving space. It's realising that our children are not mirrors of ourselves, but explorers of a world we cannot yet see. When we listen, evolve, and unlearn our need for control, we discover something far more precious: connection. True letting go is not about losing them — it's about releasing the illusion that they must be who we once were.

The future doesn't need our nostalgia; it needs them, and it needs us, walking beside them as they grow into who they are meant to be.

CHAPTER 13:
GUARDRAILS NOT GATEKEEPERS

We are not just living in a digital age — we are raising children in one. Whether you're a parent helping with homework or a teacher adapting to new tools, one truth is clear: our role in a child's digital life has never been more important.

AI is not something to block; it's something to guide. Adults are not gatekeepers who lock doors, but guardrails who keep young learners safe as they learn to navigate.

When some students say "no" to technology, it isn't laziness or lack of interest — it's often overwhelming. That makes sense. The adolescent brain — especially the prefrontal cortex, which manages decision-making, planning, and emotional regulation — is still developing. The cognitive load of deciding what to ask, what to trust, and how to use AI responsibly can feel exhausting. One antidote to this overload is Socratic thinking — teaching children to ask sharper, more focused questions rather than drowning in endless answers. By shifting the emphasis from volume to quality, we give students a way to manage the flood of information and reclaim a sense of control.

Parents can model this at home in simple ways. For example, if a child asks AI, "Tell me everything about climate change," and is hit with a wall of text, a parent might guide them to reframe the prompt: "What are the top three causes of climate change that affect Australia most directly?" The narrower, Socratic-style question produces a manageable, meaningful answer. Over time, children begin to see that the key to thriving with AI is not asking for more information, but asking for better information.

So when students push back, they're not rejecting learning. They're signaling that they need scaffolding, structure, and support. And that's where we step in—not to take control, but to guide, encourage, and build their confidence until they can drive on their own.

The Ethics of AI: What Parents Need to Know

Yes, students could use AI to cheat. Just like they could Google answers. Or copy from a friend. The issue isn't the tool—it's the values we teach around it.

Teaching students how to:

- Ask clear questions
- Verify information
- Identify when AI should not be used

These aren't bonus skills. They're essentials. Future employers won't just want knowledge—they'll want young people who can collaborate ethically with AI to solve real problems.

As Dr Darren Gray says:

"AI is only as smart as the question you ask. When we teach students to ask better questions, we're strengthening executive function — skills like planning, evaluating, and creative thinking."

CLARITY: A Framework for Smart, Ethical Prompting

To help students become thoughtful users of AI, we use the acronym CLARITY to build intention, focus, and ethical awareness into every interaction.

What is a Prompt?

A prompt is any instruction, question, or input you give to an AI system such as ChatGPT or Gemini. It is the way you tell the AI what you want it to do — whether that's answering a question, generating an idea, or creating a piece of writing.

- Example: "Explain photosynthesis to a 12-year-old in less than 100 words."

Prompt Engineering, Literacy and Fluency

- Prompt Engineering is the skill of designing and refining prompts so that an AI system produces accurate, useful, and creative responses. It is a technical skill, often used by researchers, developers, or advanced users. In class I can often gauge a student's real understanding through their prompt engineering, the way they frame questions, refine instructions, and direct an AI tool reveals the depth of their content knowledge and how clearly they understand the task. Students who are unsure of a concept tend to engage with AI the same way they once engaged with Google. They simply type the question from the worksheet or assessment task word-for-word, because they don't yet understand what is actually being asked of them. Their prompt isn't a question, it is a copy-and-paste. This difference is telling. It shows which students are thinking, analysing and shaping the inquiry and which students are still trying to find the edges of the task. That's why prompt engine engineering must now be taught as a core thinking skill not a technical add-on. When we teach students how to break apart a question, identify the key concepts, name the purpose of the and choose the right level of detail for a prompt, we are actually teaching metacognition. We are helping them think about their thoughts. Effective prompts require student students to analyse, synthesize, sequence, and clarify very skills that underpin deep learning. When we model this explicitly and when we guide them to refine a prompt step-by-step, they begin to see that AI doesn't do the thinking for them, it mirrors the clarity of the thinking they bring. That's where the real learning happens.

Artificial Intelligence can only meet the child at the level of their own understanding

- Prompt Literacy is the everyday ability to understand how prompts shape AI responses and to use them thoughtfully, ethically, and effectively. It's about teaching students (and ourselves) to be clear, critical, and intentional when working with AI. AI literacy is the starting point, the ability to understand what AI is, how it works, and how to use it safely and ethically. It's the baseline every child needs: knowing how to question an output, checkHow do you?accuracy, identify bias, and use AI as a tool rather than a shortcut. But in a world where AI will be woven into every profession, literacy is no longer enough.

- AI fluency goes further. Fluency is the ability to think with AI, to create, iterate, problem-solve, and collaborate with these tools in sophisticated ways. It's not just knowing what AI can do, but understanding when to use it, how to direct it, and how to evaluate its limitations. Fluency allows children to move beyond consuming AI-generated content to shaping it, improving it, and applying it creatively and ethically in real-world contexts. Where AI literacy asks, "Do I understand this tool?" AI fluency asks, "Can I use this tool to think better, design better, and make better decisions?" Fluency is what will differentiate children who simply keep up from those who are equipped to lead, innovate, and shape the future.

Our job as teachers now is to ensure AI is used to make students smarter and more engaged, not dull their thinking or disconnect them from their world. We must guide them to use AI to amplify their abilities, not replace them, so their human strengths continue to grow rather than fade.

The CLARITY Framework

Each time you prompt an AI, it needs guidance. CLARITY provides a checklist to help students structure their prompts:

- Context – What does the AI need to know?
  (e.g., "This is for a Year 9 student revising for a science test.")
- Limitations – What should be avoided?
  (e.g., "Avoid jargon. Keep it under 100 words.")
- Audience – Who is the response for?
  (e.g., "A 12-year-old learning about World War I.")
- Request – What exactly do you want?
  (e.g., "List the causes in bullet points.")

- Illustration – Give an example.
  (e.g., "Include militarism and alliances.")
- Tone – What tone should the answer use?
  (e.g., "Friendly but factual.")
- Yield – What output format do you need?
  (e.g., "A short paragraph, a table, or a step-by-step list.")

Why CLARITY Matters

CLARITY helps students avoid vague or misleading prompts. It encourages them to slow down, plan, and think critically. It's not just about asking better questions—it's about becoming better thinkers and ethical digital citizens.

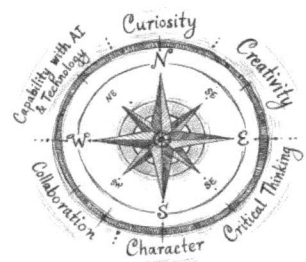

From Silence to Speaking: A Story of Kai

Kai was a quiet Year 9 student in my Japanese class. Not disruptive—just disengaged. He had already decided not to continue the subject next year. Then I introduced a text-to-speech tool. We used the CLARITY framework to guide our AI prompts.

Kai typed:

- Context: I'm learning basic Japanese phrases.
- Limitations: Speak slowly and use beginner vocabulary.
- Audience: I'm 14 years old, learning pronunciation.
- Request: Translate and say aloud the phrase "Can I have the bill, please?"
- Illustration: A native speaker's version.
- Tone: Friendly and polite.
- Yield: Hiragana, romaji, and audio only.

He clicked play. Then again. Then again. Slowly, he began mimicking the AI voice. Whispering at first. Then speaking aloud.

For the first time all term, Kai participated.

This wasn't cheating. It was scaffolded confidence. His brain was processing modelled speech, activating mirror neurons, and regulating emotional stress by removing the fear of public embarrassment. This is what guardrails look like.

The Emotional Cost of Overhelping

In our rush to help children "keep up" with technology, many adults fall into the trap of doing too much. Parents often prompt the AI for their child, or complete part of the task, just to get through the night. Teachers sometimes pre-generate ideas to "speed things up" or compensate for low confidence. But overhelping comes at a hidden cost: it chips away at student agency.

Research on executive function and learner self-efficacy tells us that growth requires ownership. When students don't learn how to struggle through unclear AI responses, revise prompts, or reframe a question, they don't build digital resilience. They become dependent, not capable.

The goal is not perfection. It's progress. When we shift our role from fixer to coach, we empower children to navigate AI with growing independence. We ask:

- What do you want help with?
- What have you already tried?
- What could you change in the prompt to get closer?

These questions build not just tech skills, but self-trust. Because ultimately, the tool should not think for the child. It should think about it with them.

Learning from Global Leaders: A Look Beyond Our Backyard

Around the world, education systems are embracing AI literacy with urgency and creativity. In China, primary-aged students are introduced to coding, robotics, and AI logic through play-based learning. The government has embedded AI curriculum objectives as early as Year 3, recognising that digital fluency is a civic skill, not a specialist one.

Singapore is rolling out AI literacy at scale through their National AI Strategy. Schools integrate discussions about ethics, data bias, and digital citizenship alongside technical skill-building. Finland, known for its progressive pedagogy, is teaching "algorithmic thinking" not just in STEM, but in subjects like HSIE and English — inviting students to reflect on how AI shapes societies, not just tasks.

Australia risks falling behind, not just in access, but in awareness. As the digital divide grows, children with confident digital mentors (whether at home or school) will thrive. Those without them may fall further behind.

This is why parent partnership matters more than ever. You don't need to code. You need to care. You need to stay curious. You need to ask questions beside your child, not just answer them.

Global research shows us that equity in AI starts with relationships. When families and schools co-manage this space with openness and ethical clarity, children build the mindset to shape technology, not be shaped by it.

The Emotional Dimension

Using AI isn't just cognitive. It's emotional.

Students feel pressure to keep up. They fear being accused of cheating. They worry they're not doing things "the right way."

When we create space to explore AI tools with safety and reflection, we reduce anxiety and increase emotional regulation. We build emotional intelligence.

And that matters.

In the age of automation, emotional intelligence is a competitive advantage. Skills like empathy, resilience, self-awareness, and ethical reasoning will set students apart in a world where knowledge is searchable.

Empowering, Not Replacing Learning

AI doesn't replace teaching. Or thinking. It complements both.

When students are:

- Curious
- Reflective
- Willing to experiment

AI becomes a catalyst.

But only if we also value:

- Summarising
- Synthesising
- Collaborating
- Explaining ideas aloud
- Revising and refining

The best classrooms use AI as a scaffold, not a shortcut. Students can use it to brainstorm or rehearse — but the final work still belongs to them.

What Parents and Teachers Can Do Now

Here are 6 practical ways to put guardrails in place:

1. **Teach Prompt Literacy**

Use CLARITY to help students ask better questions. Their CLARITY demonstrates their understanding.

2. **Celebrate Process, Not Just Product**

    Ask students to reflect: "What did AI help you with? What did you have to do yourself?"

3. **Have Open Ethical Conversations**

    Ask: "When is AI helpful? When might it cross a line? What does responsible use look like?"

4. **Let Curiosity Lead**

    Encourage play. Let them try silly prompts. Then talk about the limits and implications.

5. **Model at Home**

    Say things like:

    - "That AI answer gave me a good starting point. Now I'll put it in my own words."
    - "It didn't get it quite right. I'm going to adjust the prompt."

6. **Create a Family Tech Agreement**

Together, decide:

- When AI can be used

- When it shouldn't be
- How to share what was learned from it

Everyday Examples of Guardrails in Action

- Homework Help: Your child pastes an AI-generated paragraph. Ask: "What would you add or change to make this sound like your voice?"
- Screen-Time Conflict: Your teen wants more time using AI. Say: "Show me one way you used it to solve a problem this week."
- In the Staffroom: A teacher says, "I used AI to plan my lesson." You respond, "How did you adapt it for your learners?"

These aren't just conversations. They're coaching moments.

Reflection Questions for Parents and Educators

- How is AI being framed in our home or school: as a threat or a tool?
- What values do I want my children or students to carry into the digital world?

- When did I last model ethical AI use?
- How might I involve my child in shaping our family's tech boundaries?

Final Thought

AI will not replace teachers, it will amplify the impact of those who know how to use it wisely.

Our job isn't to raise kids who can just use AI.

It's to raise kids who use it with integrity, empathy, imagination, and purpose.

Let's stop asking how to ban it.

Let's start asking how to teach it well.

Let's walk beside our children, not behind them.

Let's trade gatekeeping for CLARITY.

Because the future won't belong to the fastest adopters.

It will belong to the wisest navigators.

CHAPTER 14:
THE NEW GRANDPARENTING – CO-PARENTS, NOT JUST CARERS

When my sister and I had our first children just three weeks apart, our parents faced a choice. They were still living in Tasmania, close to their own friends and networks, but far from us. To stay would mean being occasional visitors in their grandchildren's lives — the kind of grandparents who swoop in for birthdays and Christmas, perhaps the odd school concert, but who aren't there for the everyday moments that matter most.

My parents knew what they wanted. They had watched me grow up in Burnie with grandparents woven into the fabric of daily life. My grandparents lived at "The Shack" in Cowrie Point near Rocky Cape, Tasmania. Summers there smelled of salt and suncream.

My grandfather, Pa or "Curl" was a clearance diver in the Australian Navy and was formidable in both presence and principle. He was determined his granddaughters would be tough, capable, and unafraid of challenge. We were "Curl's granddaughters," and that name carried weight in the close-knit diving community. He made sure we learned to swim, fish and to dive — not because it was easy, but because it was part of his legacy. My grandmother, equally strong, worked for Edgell Farms and was known for her discipline and tireless work ethic. They raised us on a diet of hard work, resilience, and expectation. That was our inheritance.

That same work ethic was instilled by my parents. My mother carried it into surf life saving, breaking barriers as Australia's first female state president and later securing millions of dollars in government grants to build not one but two new surf clubs — Burnie, Tasmania and Bonny Hills, NSW. My father's discipline was forged early. He was raised on a farm and lost his own father when he was just twenty-one. From that point, responsibility was not optional — it was survival. He went on to build a life of grit and independence, running his own businesses, including trucks and the Cooee Newsagency, before moving into a kind of semi-retirement driving for Cadbury Chocolates. The ongoing joke in our family is that this was the real reason Darren asked me to marry him — a lifetime supply of chocolate delivered straight from the source.

Behind the humour, though, was a serious truth. These stories taught us that effort, determination, and service were non-negotiable. These were the standards he and Mum lived by, and they were the standards they passed on to us. When they became grandparents, those same values became the bedrock of how they co-parented — steady, united and always anchored in hard work and love.

Darren grew up in a home that balanced discipline with plenty of warmth and care. His dad was a Principal and later director of State based tertiary vocational training college, deeply committed to education and also heavily involved in the Scouting movement, which was thriving through the 1980s. He had a way of encouraging young people to push themselves, give back, and discover just how much they were capable of. Darren's mum, meanwhile, made their house a safe and steady place for four kids to grow. When the time felt right, she stepped back into work as a bank teller — bringing the same patience and kindness she'd always shown at home.

Darren's grandparents lived in Sydney. Travelling to Sydney back then was a long 7-8 hr car drive from their family home Sawtell, on the north coast of NSW. The distance meant that visits were precious, gathered mostly around Christmas and school holidays. Those times became woven into memory — days filled with laughter, tradition, and the feeling of being held close, even if only for a while. Yet the spaces in between also taught him something — the difference between grandparents who are part of the everyday and those whose presence is treasured in moments. That gentle contrast has stayed with Darren and continues to shape how he values the unique and irreplaceable role of grandparents and carers in family life today.

When my parents looked at their grandchildren, they knew distance wasn't an option. They wanted to be there not just for milestones but for the Monday-to-Friday rhythms: after-school drop-ins, cheering at Saturday sport, sleepovers that became traditions. They wanted their grandchildren to grow up with grandparents not on the periphery but at the centre of their lives. So they packed up, brought my grandmother with them, and moved closer.

What followed was not babysitting. It was co-parenting.

The Changing Shape of Families

Across the world, this story is repeating. The traditional image of grandparents as the occasional providers of treats and stories is fading. Today, many are woven into the very fabric of raising children. They manage school runs, reinforce rules, guide homework, and in some cases, provide the stability that keeps households afloat.

Why? Because families are under pressure. The cost of living continues to climb. More women are in full-time work than ever before, and rightly so — we are still on the long road to closing the gender pay gap. But equality on paper doesn't solve the practical challenge: someone still needs to be with the children. In many families, that "someone" is a grandparent or a trusted carer.

This isn't just about economics. It's about culture. Families want their children raised in love, not left in systems that feel impersonal or stretched. Grandparents often step in, not only because they're available, but because they carry the family values, discipline, and continuity that parents long to preserve.

But this shift has consequences. Grandparents are no longer just caring. They are co-parenting. And with that comes both opportunity and strain.

The Digital Divide

The biggest change between the way grandparents once raised children and the way they now co-parent is the presence of technology. When they raised us, the biggest parenting debates were about television or curfews. Today, the conversations are about Roblox, gaming, social media, and in general, devices that never leave a child's hand.

Many grandparents feel unprepared for this new terrain. They may be masters of discipline, of work ethic, of community responsibility — but as digital immigrants, they did not grow up with smartphones or AI tutors. The language of apps, platforms, and algorithms can feel foreign.

Children, on the other hand, are digital natives. They move through devices and platforms with ease. This imbalance can leave grandparents unsure. Should they say yes to another hour on the iPad? Should they allow AI homework tools? Should they trust the game their grandchild insists "everyone is playing"?

These questions are not minor. They are daily decisions with long-term consequences. And they are questions that grandparents cannot afford to ignore, because their role is no longer on the sidelines.

The Neuroscience of Boundaries and Consistency Across Development

From infancy through adolescence, the brain undergoes rapid and prolonged development. In the early years, neural circuits responsible for emotional regulation, attachment, and sensory integration were highly plastic, making them particularly sensitive to the consistency of caregiving environments. As children progress into adolescence, the prefrontal cortex — the centre of executive function and self-regulation — continues to mature, with synaptic pruning and myelination extending well into the early twenties.

Boundaries and predictable routines act as stabilising inputs for this developmental process. When parents, grandparents, and other caregivers present a unified approach to expectations — such as sleep schedules, nutrition, screen use, or social behaviour — the child's brain encounters coherence.

This stability reduces stress-related activation of the hypothalamic-pituitary-adrenal (HPA) axis and strengthens neural pathways that underpin resilience, emotional balance, and decision-making capacity.

Inconsistent rules across caregivers, however, create cognitive dissonance. The brain is forced to navigate conflicting signals, increasing cognitive load and undermining the consolidation of self-regulation skills. For younger children, this may manifest as emotional volatility; for adolescents, as risk-taking or resistance to authority. In both cases, unpredictability can weaken the developmental trajectory of the prefrontal cortex, delaying the acquisition of long-term planning and impulse control.

Grandparents and other caregivers therefore hold a biologically significant role. Their reinforcement of parental boundaries does more than "keep the peace" — it directly shapes the neuroarchitecture of developing brains. By aligning with parents, they provide continuity across environments, fostering security, confidence, and the neurological foundations for lifelong wellbeing.

More Than Babysitting: The Emotional Stakes

Being a co-parent is more than enforcing rules. It is about being present in ways that shape identity. For many children, their relationship with grandparents or carers becomes a stabilising force. They know who will be at the soccer match. They know where they can go after school. They know whose voice will say, "Homework first, then games."

But with this comes tension. Grandparents may worry about being too strict, or conversely, being seen as too lenient. They may fear undermining the parents or being judged by them. They may struggle with their own confidence around technology, worried that they will "get it wrong."

The truth is, none of this is easy. But children benefit most when all adults in their lives work in harmony. Parents, grandparents, and carers need to see themselves as a team, not as competing voices.

Bridging Generations Through AI

While AI may feel daunting, it can also become a bridge between generations. Imagine a grandparent sitting beside a grandchild, saying, "Show me how this works." Suddenly, the child is the teacher, the expert. That role reversal is powerful. It validates the child's knowledge and curiosity, while allowing the grandparent to learn without fear.

I have seen families use AI to co-create bedtime stories, plan trips together, or even generate recipes with the ingredients in the fridge. The laughter, the sense of discovery — it is the same as baking together or building a cubby house, only in a new form. Technology, when approached with openness, doesn't erode tradition. It extends it.

*Children often walk further when it's a grandparent beside them —
someone who listens, steadies, and never judges.*

Lessons from Crowrie Point, Tasmania

When I think back to my own childhood, the lessons from my grandparents are clear. From *"The Shack"* at

Rocky Cape, Tasmania, I learned that hard work wasn't optional — it was simply part of who we were. Pa, my grandfather's insistence we scuba dive wasn't just about sport; it was about facing challenges head-on and discovering what we were capable of. My grandmother's dedication at Edgell Farms showed us the quiet pride of doing a job well, along with the value of planning and patience.

Pa always had us up at the crack of dawn. We'd pile into the boat, still half asleep, to go and check the cray pots and nets. It was just what you did — no excuses. On the way back, just when my sister and I thought we were finished, Pa would pull up at a buoy he'd anchored offshore. That was our cue. Over the side we'd go, straight into the freezing waters of Tasmania, and swim all the way back to shore. At the time, we hated every second of it — the shock of the cold, the scary seaweed, the currents that always seemed against us. But we'll never forget it. And truthfully, I wouldn't take it back for the world. Those mornings taught us determination, perseverance, and a whole lot of lessons we didn't even know we were learning at the time.

Those lessons live on. They taught me that family is built in the everyday — in the discipline of showing up, in the pride of belonging to a community, and in the willingness to step into what feels unfamiliar. Today, grandparents and carers face a different kind of ocean to dive into: the digital one. It can feel cold and intimidating. But the principle is the same. With discipline, curiosity, and a steady hand, they can find their place and guide the next generation safely through.

Grandparent's Toolkit for the AI Age - Ideas to explore together, not instructions to follow.

Grandparents and carers don't need lessons in raising children — they've already done that. What they often need instead is a way to feel confident stepping into this new digital space without losing the traditions and rhythms that make their role so important. One of the simplest and most effective approaches is to use AI not as a replacement for their wisdom, but as a spark for shared experiences.

AI can become a conversation starter, a playful collaborator, or even a bridge between the old and the new. For example, you might sit down with your grandchild and ask AI to write a bedtime story with them as the main character, complete with their dog or guinea pig cast as the sidekick. Read it together, laugh at the details, and maybe even act it out afterwards. In another moment, you could share a memory from your own childhood — like Pa making us jump into the icy waters off Tasmania after checking the cray pots — and then ask AI to retell that story as a poem, or a cartoon adventure. The comparison often leads to laughter and deeper conversations about what really happened and what it taught you.

AI can also be wonderfully practical. Imagine the grandkids using it to plan a surprise "date night restaurant" at home after a long day at work for Mum and Dad. They might ask AI to help design an invitation in Canva, suggest a seafood menu, and even generate simple recipes. Once the ideas are on the table, the kids can take charge — setting the table like a real restaurant, preparing dishes with a little help, and presenting the evening as their very own creation. In this way, technology isn't just a screen — it becomes a launchpad for memory-making, turning ordinary family time into something special and unforgettable.

Importantly, AI can help shift time off screens too. It can be asked to design a mystery treasure hunt around the house or garden, where each clue involves a riddle, a code to crack, or even a maths puzzle that sends the children racing from room to room. It can suggest recipes based on a photograph of the contents of the fridge — but with a twist, like setting a "masterchef-style challenge" where kids have to swap an ingredient, invent a new dish, and then vote on their favourite creation.

AI can even generate a "choose-your-own-adventure" scavenger list for a bushwalk or trip to the park: not just "find a feather" but "find something that could float, something that feels rough, and something that reminds you of home." This encourages observation, creativity, and storytelling when they share their finds.

Other possibilities? AI can help children invent a brand-new board game using whatever household objects are lying around — then play it as a family. It can create logic puzzles where kids become detectives solving a "family mystery." Or it can help them plan a mini "escape room" at home, with locks, riddles, and challenges that parents have to solve to "escape" the lounge room.

These activities don't just entertain; they stretch imagination, encourage teamwork, and build problem-solving skills. And most importantly, they create memories of laughter, curiosity, and connection that will last far longer than the AI that sparked them.

For older grandchildren, AI can provide even more tailored opportunities. Teenage girls, for example, are often immersed in fashion and makeup culture. Instead of simply scrolling through endless online tutorials, AI can be used to create something collaborative. A professional makeup artist recently explained that she uses AI to generate "face charts" — digital images showing how makeup will look on a face. Because makeup doesn't translate well onto paper, these charts are far more realistic and professional, and they save time. Grandparents can invite their granddaughters to design a look together, print it out, and then use it as a guide for experimenting at home. It becomes both creative and practical — a chance to blend art, technology, and play.

Teenage boys, on the other hand, might prefer AI as a sports coach. You could sit down with them and ask AI to design a basketball or soccer training session that can be done in the backyard using whatever's on hand — a rubbish bin for a hoop, cones made from plastic bottles, or a ball retrieved from the shed. Then you can head outside together to run through the drills. It's not about perfection; it's about movement, creativity, and connection.

Sometimes the challenge for grandparents is knowing how to connect with older grandchildren whose worlds feel so different. Here, AI can help spark questions that show genuine interest. You might ask it to generate conversation starters about their favourite games: "How do you know who's on your team in NBA 2K?" or "What makes a good strategy in Minecraft?" From there, you can let your grandchild explain, and you'll be surprised how much they open up when they're the expert.

AI can also suggest questions about shared activities: "What's something you've built online with your friends?" or "If you could design a challenge for others, what would it be?" These aren't just small talk — they invite storytelling, creativity, and connection on the things that matter most to young people.

The truth is, what children will remember isn't the AI itself. They'll remember the way their guinea pig became a superhero in a story, the pasta dish you cooked together, the scavenger hunt in the backyard, the makeup look you designed and tried, or the soccer drills you ran in the driveway. AI is not the destination — it's just another tool to help grandparents and carers do what they have always done best: create memories, pass on values, and spend time together in ways that matter.

AI-Powered Prompts for Connecting with Older Grandchildren

Gaming & Esports

1. "Generate three thoughtful questions I could ask my grandchild about NBA 2K that show genuine curiosity about how teamwork works in the game."

2. "Suggest conversation starters about Minecraft builds that would let my grandchild teach me what they've created or designed."

Music & Creativity

3. "Give me questions to ask my grandchild about their Spotify playlists — what makes a great playlist, how they discover new artists, and which songs matter to them most."

4. "Suggest ways I could connect with my grandchild if they are producing beats or writing music, even though I don't know the software."

Sport & Fitness

5. "Create prompts I can use to talk with my grandchild about their sport (e.g., basketball, soccer, netball) — questions that go deeper than 'Did you win?'"

6. "Suggest ways I could ask my grandchild to teach me a simple drill or warm-up they use at training."

Fashion & Style

7. "Give me questions to ask my teenage granddaughter about fashion trends on TikTok or Instagram that will show interest without sounding critical."

8. "Suggest activities we could do together using AI — like designing outfits on Canva or an AI art platform — that connect to her love of style."

STEM & Tech

9. "Generate questions I can ask my grandchild about coding or robotics projects — ways to invite them to explain their thinking."

10. "Suggest collaborative AI projects we could do if my grandchild enjoys technology—like building a digital scavenger hunt or designing a simple game."

Life & Social Interests

11. "Create reflective questions I can ask my grandchild about what's important to them in their friendships or online communities."

12. "Suggest ways I can ask about their future goals or dreams that feel supportive and curious rather than pressuring."

These prompts do two things:

- They position the grandchild as the expert (so they can teach and explain).
- They show authentic curiosity from grandparents, moving beyond "How was school?" into deeper conversations.

Reflections for Grandparents and Carers

Ask yourself: Am I a helper, or am I a co-parent? Do I feel confident in supporting my grandchildren's digital lives, or do I need to learn more? How can I bring the values of resilience, work ethic, and care that shaped me into this new digital world?

Remember, your wisdom is not made redundant by technology. AI can answer questions, but it cannot pass on discipline. It cannot cheer on the sidelines. It cannot tell the story of how your grandfather was a Navy diver, or how your mother broke barriers in surf life saving. That is your legacy, and it matters.

Final Thought

The role of grandparents and carers has changed, but its essence has not. It is still about love, presence, and guidance. What has shifted is the scope: no longer occasional, it is daily. No longer confined to tradition, it now stretches into the digital age.

Grandparents and carers are not just keeping children safe while parents work. They are raising them — alongside, in partnership, and with as much influence as anyone else. By embracing this role with confidence and openness, they ensure that children grow up not only digitally fluent, but deeply grounded in the values that make us human.

PART FOUR: DIFFERENT MINDS, SAME FUTURE

CHAPTER 15:
WIRED DIFFERENTLY – AI AND CHILDREN WITH LEARNING DIFFERENCES

The Invisible Work of Love — What Parents of Children with Learning Differences Quietly Do

To the parent who's tired of IEP (Individual Education Plan) meetings, who dreads the sight of the school's phone number on their phone, who worries everyday about the emotional state their child will arrive home in each and every day.

You're not failing. You're showing up in ways no one sees. The fact that you're reading this means you're already giving your child a gift most kids never get: belief, patience, and love. This chapter isn't about perfection—

it's about possibility. There is a future where your child can learn, thrive, and even lead. We're just building a new path to get there. Together.

Some of the most powerful acts of parenting are the ones no one sees. Behind every child navigating the world with a learning difference, there is usually a parent quietly shaping that journey — reworking, translating, scripting, buffering, and cheering — without recognition or reprieve.

They don't do it for praise. They do it for survival, belonging, and hope.

In the age of AI and rising academic pressure, the gap between what's expected and what's possible for neurodivergent children can feel impossibly wide. That's where parents step in — not as rule-breakers, but as lifelines. Here are just some of the invisible acts of devotion many parents perform every day.

1. They Do the Homework (But Feel Guilty About It)

It often begins innocently. A late-night project, a misunderstood instruction, a worksheet that assumes too much. Parents sit beside their child — and then gradually take over. Not because they want to cheat the system, but because they know their child understands — they just can't output at the level expected.

They hit submit. Then feel the weight of guilt, knowing it was their brain, not their child's, on that screen.

2. They Secretly Learn the Subject Too

To support their child, many parents become accidental students. They learn Japanese so they can write vocab flashcards. They watch YouTube math tutorials to help explain trigonometry in plain English. They Google "How to explain metaphors to a 12-year-old with ADHD."

They do this, not to helicopter — but to scaffold. Because sometimes the schoolwork assumes a level of independence their child just doesn't yet have.

3. They Edit Social Realities

When your child is socially vulnerable, you become their PR team. Parents read the group chats, delete hurtful comments, "accidentally" forget to mention parties their child wasn't invited to. They tell white lies to protect fragile hearts. "No one's really going." "I think that was just for older kids."

It's not a deception. It's emotional triage.

4. They Coach Every Social Interaction

Before a party, camp, or even a sleepover, some parents spend hours role-playing with their child:

- What to say when someone ignores you.
- How to ask to join a game.
- When to leave a conversation that feels off.

Afterward, they debrief like sports analysts: "What went well? What felt hard? Let's try it differently next time."

They are teaching not just social skills — but social resilience.

5. They Cry in Private — Often

The hardest truth? Parents often collapse at the end of the day — on the kitchen floor, in the shower, in the driver's seat of the car. Not because they're weak — but because they're doing everything to keep their child strong.

The tears aren't just from exhaustion. They're from watching a child constantly misunderstood, constantly trying, constantly falling short of a system that wasn't built for them.

6. They Advocate Like Warriors — But Hide the Battles

Most people don't see the emails, the school meetings, the National Assessment Program Language And Numeracy (NAPLAN) reports, the doctors appointments, the waitlists, the assessments, the arguments with insurance, the late-night Googling of strategies and support plans.

They don't know how many times the parent had to hold their tongue when someone said, "He just needs to focus more" or "She's so bright, she just doesn't apply herself."

But parents know. They always know. And they keep going.

These hidden acts aren't small. They are monumental.. They change the course of a child's life.

So if you are one of these parents — know this:

You are not alone. You are not weak. You are not doing it wrong.

You are doing what love looks like when systems fail to see the whole child.

And in this AI-powered future, where tools can offer support but not soul, your presence is still the most powerful intervention there is.

Because no technology can replicate what you do. Not now. Not ever.

When the Teacher Isn't There: Self-Differentiation for Life

Parents and employers often have no idea just how much differentiation takes place in the everyday life of a classroom. It isn't just about assessments—it's every lesson, every worksheet, every explanation. Teachers constantly adjust the way they present content: shifting the language, breaking tasks into steps, re-framing questions, offering visual scaffolds, or providing alternative examples. This invisible work happens minute by minute and is one of the greatest acts of professional skill. But once students step into the workforce, that scaffolding often vanishes. Employers don't typically differentiate—and in most cases, they don't know how.

The danger is that we raise young people who've always had others adapt for them, but never learned how to adapt for themselves. That's why we must explicitly teach students how to differentiate their own world: how to change the way they receive information, how to adjust inputs to match their learning style, and how to advocate for what they need. When they can do this, they don't just cope—they flourish. They show up as their authentic selves, and that is exactly what the world needs. Not another robot, but unique thinkers who know how to shine.

From a neuroscience perspective, this matters deeply. Darren often explains that the brain is shaped by neuroplasticity—its ability to reorganise itself in response to experience. When students learn to switch input channels (from text to speech, from images to words, from structured lists to visual maps), they are literally building flexible neural pathways. This adaptability strengthens executive function, working memory, and resilience under pressure. In other words, teaching children to self-differentiate is not just an academic skill—it's brain training for life.

Three Ways to Practise Self-Differentiation at Home

1. Experiment with Input Formats

    Encourage your child to learn the same material in different ways: read an article, listen to it read aloud with text-to-speech, or sketch a diagram of the key points. Afterwards, ask: Which one made it clearest for you? This builds awareness of their own learning pathways.

2. Model Self-Advocacy

    When your child feels stuck, prompt them to ask for what they need rather than jumping in to fix it. Phrases like: "Can you explain that more simply?" or "Can you show me an example?" build the neural and social habit of advocacy, which they will need beyond school.

3. Build a Personal Toolkit

    Work with your child to create a visible set of tools that match their style — such as voice typing, colour overlays, mind maps, or breaking tasks into timed chunks. This "learning toolkit" makes differentiation normal, practical, and empowering, rather than secret or remedial.

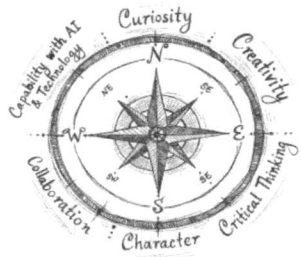

Everyday Advocacy: A Year 10 Social Justice Breakthrough

In my Year 10 Religion class, we were exploring the theme of Social Justice in Action. Students were tasked with designing a multi-modal campaign to raise awareness of a current social issue — anything from refugee resettlement to domestic violence, poverty, or environmental justice.

The brief was intentionally open-ended: choose an issue, research it, and present it using any combination of spoken word, video, infographics, or digital storytelling. Some students took off with Canva and Gemini. Others storyboarded video ideas or drafted spoken word monologues.

But one student — Luca — froze.

He's the kind of student who has powerful opinions in class discussions. He cares deeply about equity. He speaks with passion. But when it came time to pull his ideas into a product, he sat quietly, staring at the blank page.

The Power of Partnership

Later that week, I received an email from his dad:

"Luca's stuck. He's tried to start three times. He really wants to do it, but I think he's just overwhelmed. Is there another way to tackle this?"

I suggested a few gentle entry points:

- Use Gemini or ChatGPT to break the topic into manageable chunks.
- Try voice typing to brainstorm aloud rather than writing from scratch.

- Prompt the AI with: "Give me five angles for a social justice campaign on homelessness."

His dad responded the next day:

"We sat together and tried it. Once he saw the ideas broken down, he ran with it. He used voice typing to get started and then built a carousel post for Instagram. He's actually excited to finish it."

On presentation day, Luca's work stood out. His three-part campaign on youth homelessness featured clear facts, a call-to-action, and visuals he created using DALL·E prompts - an AI modelling converting text to images. He explained how he tailored the tone for a teenage audience:

"I wanted it to feel like something I'd actually post."

It wasn't just polished — it was powerful. And it all began with one moment of everyday advocacy — a parent sitting beside their child, asking, *"Want to try a different way?"*

AI: A Bridge for Different Brains

Luca's story is not an outlier. In my role as a HALT-accredited teacher, I've worked with colleagues to reimagine learning environments using digital tools like Diffit, Gemini, Perplexity and Google Read&Write — especially for students with ADHD, dyslexia, anxiety, autism, and other neurodivergent profiles.

Traditional classrooms pose many hidden barriers: the speed of instruction, the pressure to output quickly, the fear of judgment, and inconsistent scaffolding. These can exhaust or shut down a student before they even begin.

Understanding Your Neurodivergent Child's Brain: A Parent's Guide

Our brains aren't single thinking machines — they're two specialised halves working like skilled dance partners. This hemispheric organisation shapes how we process information and see the world.

Understanding How Your Child's Brain is Organised

Brain organisation refers to how different abilities become specialised in each side of the brain as children develop. This isn't random — it's nature's smart design that allows the brain to multitask and work efficiently.

The *left side* develops as the detail specialist, with busy networks in areas that control speech and language understanding. It loves breaking things down step-by-step, processing words and grammar, and handling precise movements. Think of it as a focused torch, examining details one at a time.

The **right side** becomes the big-picture expert, with networks that understand emotional tone and spatial relationships. It processes lots of information at once, recognises feelings in faces, gets jokes and sarcasm, and understands metaphors. This side works like a floodlight, lighting up broad patterns and connections.

How the Brain Sides Talk to Each Other

The corpus callosum — a bridge containing over 200 million message-carrying fibres — lets both sides have constant conversations. This isn't just sharing information; it's smart teamwork where each side contributes its strengths and sometimes tells the other side to step back when needed. This process ensures the right thinking style takes charge for each task.

The brain also has backup communication pathways, creating multiple routes for information flow that help with flexible thinking.

Neurodivergent Hemispheric Patterns

In neurodivergent children, this brain organisation develops along different pathways, creating unique thinking styles rather than problems.

Dyslexia involves different left-side organisation, particularly in areas that normally handle sound-letter connections. Brain scans show less activity in these traditional reading areas, but increased activity in right-side visual areas. This creates enhanced abilities to see 3D relationships, better peripheral vision, and exceptional skill at understanding how things fit together in space — talents that shine in fields like architecture, engineering, and creative arts.

Autism shows unique organisation patterns where the brain recruits different areas for typical tasks. For example, face recognition might use left-side areas instead of the usual right-side networks. The communication bridge between sides often has structural differences — sometimes thicker in some areas, sometimes thinner overall — affecting how information flows between sides. This creates the characteristic ability to notice incredible details before seeing the whole picture.

ADHD involves different organisation in the front brain areas that control attention and planning. The right side's control networks show less activity, while the left side may boost its creativity networks to compensate. This creates a brain that finds sustained focus challenging but excels at flexible thinking, spotting new patterns, and finding innovative solutions—essentially trading steady attention for creative agility.

Darren, working with functional neurology supports neurodivergent students by balancing brain performance. "Understanding hemispheric differences transforms our approach. Instead of forcing conformity, we recognise each brain's natural organisation and create environments where different cognitive styles thrive," he emphasises.

Neurodivergence represents natural variations in brain lateralisation—different wiring that contributes unique strengths to human diversity.

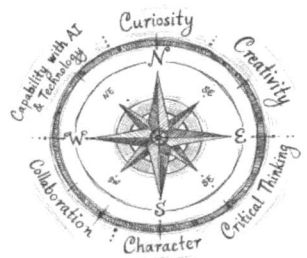

Real Stories, Real Progress

In my Year 9 Religion class, Max, a student with diagnosed dyslexia and anxiety, used Gemini to co-write a paragraph on the Beatitudes. He began by asking:

"Can you explain the Beatitudes like I'm 11?"

He smiled and said, "Now I get it." He then rewrote it in his own words—comprehension first, creation second.

Josh, who struggles with working memory, used Gemini to visually organise his thoughts for a Religious Education task. The AI scaffolded his thinking without replacing it. For the first time all term, he submitted a task on time—with pride.

AI Removes the Mask

Many neurodivergent children spend enormous energy on masking—suppressing their natural responses to fit in. The mental toll of this is immense, especially for students with autism or anxiety.

But AI offers a rare kind of safety. There's no judgment. No pressure to perform.

Josh, a quiet student with ASD, once told me: "The AI doesn't get frustrated with me. It just waits." That simple statement says everything. He could practise without panic. The learning became accessible not because it was easier—but because it was safer.

How Artificial Intelligence Changes Feedback and Revision

One of the most powerful shifts we're seeing in education is this, students are more willing to act on feedback from AI than from their teacher. Across studies from Stanford, Monash University, Harvard, and the University of Hong Kong, researchers found the same pattern:

- Students revise more frequently after AI feedback.
- They take more academic risks.
- They show greater openness to correcting errors.
- They report feeling less judged, even when they believe their teacher knows more.

When asked why, students consistently say:

- "It doesn't feel personal."
- "AI doesn't think I'm incompetent."
- "I'm not embarrassed."
- "I know my teacher will see the final version, not my messy drafts."

AI creates emotional distance — and that distance matters. It allows students to fail privately, iterate without fear, and approach revision with curiosity rather than defensiveness. The feedback isn't better. The feedback feels safer. And once safety rises, learning follows.

But this shift also creates a new challenge. Teachers must be able to see the process, not just the polished final version. Without access to the drafts, the false starts, the clarifying prompts, and the revisions made with AI, all a teacher sees is perfection — and perfection tells us nothing about a student's thinking. In reality, this means inviting students to screenshot their prompts, upload their revision history, or briefly explain the steps they took with the AI before submitting their final work. It means teachers examining how students refine a prompt, what questions they ask to clarify misunderstandings, and how their draft evolves across iterations. This transparency doesn't undermine the use of AI, it reveals the learning. AI may make revision safer, but teachers still need visibility into the messy middle where growth actually happens.

Building Self-Advocacy Through Prompting

Learning to prompt AI effectively isn't just about better answers—it's about building self-awareness and advocacy.

When a student says:

- "Can you explain that more simply?"
- "Can you show me an example with a picture?"

- "Break this into steps for me…"

They're practising how to ask for what they need — not just with a machine, but eventually with teachers, tutors, and employers.

Maya, a Year 7 student who used to shut down at the start of writing tasks, learned to scaffold her own process using AI:

"Help me brainstorm. Help me plan. I'll write it myself."

That's not dependency. That's ownership.

Customisation and Co-Regulation

Many learners need more than content differentiation — they need customised regulation:

- Text-to-speech or speech-to-text for auditory learners
- Dyslexia-friendly fonts and colour overlays
- Slower voice playback and adjustable repetition
- Visual mind maps for spatial thinkers

These features can be designed into AI interactions — transforming digital tools into personal learning allies.

Why This Matters

In an era of high-stakes assessments and standardised pace, AI allows students to reclaim something vital: dignity in learning.

It can't fix every struggle. It can't remove every barrier. But it can soften the edges, break down the task, reduce the fear, and return joy to students who've forgotten what it feels like to succeed.

Understanding How Your Child's Brain Learns Best

Darren's clinical experience gives him unique insight into how different brains adapt and thrive under the right conditions. His research into working memory — think of it as your child's mental workspace — shows us something really important: children with ADHD and processing differences have the same intellectual potential as their peers, but their brains work with a smaller "workspace" for holding and manipulating information.

When we reduce the cognitive load on this workspace through strategies like breaking tasks into smaller chunks, allowing more processing time, and providing clear, step-by-step feedback, something remarkable happens. The brain becomes more efficient, freeing up precious mental resources for higher-order thinking, creativity, and problem-solving. It's not about making things easier — it's about making them more accessible to how your child's brain naturally functions.

For children on the autism spectrum, Darren's insights highlights the crucial role of the prefrontal cortex — the brain's executive centre — and the limbic system, which processes emotions and stress responses. These neural networks function optimally when the learning environment

is predictable, structured, and free from unexpected changes.

AI platforms like ChatGPT and Perplexity create what neuroscientists call a "low-threat" environment. Their consistent tone, infinite patience with repetition, and predictable responses help keep your child's attention networks engaged rather than triggered into a stress response.

What's particularly exciting is Darren's advocacy for truly adaptive learning systems. Rather than one-size-fits-all approaches, these platforms can respond to your child's neurological state in real-time. By engaging multiple sensory pathways simultaneously—auditory processing through text-to-speech, spatial-visual networks through mind mapping, and motor-sensory integration through voice input—we're working with your child's brain architecture, not against it.

This multimodal approach strengthens neural connections across different brain regions, creating more robust learning pathways. It's about moving beyond simple accommodations to genuine neurological empowerment — giving your child not just access to learning, but the tools to learn in ways that honour how their unique brain works best.

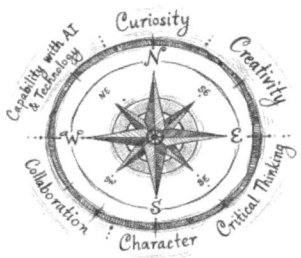

Everyday Advocacy: Finding a Voice in Japanese

In my Year 8 Japanese class, I have a student, Emi, who is selectively mute. She has never spoken a single word to me — not in English, and not in Japanese. In group tasks, she sits quietly. In oral assessments, she freezes. Her silence isn't defiance — it's fear.

But Emi is sharp. Her written work shows careful thought. She remembers vocabulary others forget. Her hiragana is immaculate. It was clear that she understood the content — but the expectation of speaking aloud built a wall she couldn't climb.

One afternoon, while the rest of the class practised dialogues in pairs, I quietly offered her a different option:

"Would you like to try it here first, with AI?"

I set up Gemini with a simple prompt: "Act like a Japanese real estate agent. Ask me what type of house I am looking for." Emi typed her answers in English, and the AI generated the Japanese for her. Then she copied the text into the voice feature and listened. She rehearsed silently, mouthing the words with her headphones in.

Later, she used the text-to-speech tool to "speak" her dialogue back to the AI. For the first time, she completed an oral task — without saying a word out loud. Her face lit up. It wasn't about bypassing her silence — it was about giving her a safe rehearsal space where she could participate without panic.

Over the term, something shifted. Emi began recording short snippets of her own voice, starting with single words. Then a phrase. Finally, one day, she quietly whispered an answer to me in class. It was just a few syllables—but it was hers.

Her mum emailed later that week:

"She came home and said, 'I actually spoke in Japanese today.' We cried. Thank you for finding a way that made her feel safe enough to try."

AI didn't cure her mutism. It didn't erase her anxiety. But it gave her a bridge—a safe step toward being heard on her own terms. For Emi, that single whispered phrase was not small. It was monumental.

Parent Wins That Deserve Recognition

- You explained the same homework instruction five times—with kindness.
- You remembered their noise-cancelling headphones on an excursion.
- You emailed the teacher, again, to advocate.
- You celebrated effort, not just grades.
- You cried in the car but smiled at the pickup.

- These are not small things. They are everything.

What You Can Do as a Parent

- Let your child explore tools like voice typing, visual mind maps (egNOTEGPT), and simplified summarisation. They're not shortcuts—they're scaffolds.
- Ask: "Which parts do you want the tool to help with—and which parts do you want to try solo?
- Celebrate small wins in independence and confidence, not just output.
- Encourage exploration without pressure—AI tools can respond without judgement or urgency.

Try This:

- Explore AI-generated diagrams or timelines together to clarify key ideas.
- Help your child build their own "toolkit" of AI supports tailored to their thinking and learning style.
- Use voice prompts or screen readers for students who process information better aurally.

- Set up a co-working space at home where your child can use AI with you nearby—not as a supervisor, but as a supportive ally.

Final Thought

Differentiation in the classroom must be normalised as a cornerstone of educational practice, ensuring that every learner's unique pathway is not only accommodated but actively valued. Effective differentiation acknowledges that students have distinct strengths, backgrounds, and learning styles, making one-size-fits-all instruction obsolete. When instruction is personalised and responsive, all learners—regardless of their starting point—are better equipped to reach their potential without fear of stigma or comparison.

Embedding and normalising differentiated instruction is a mark of professional accountability and high-quality teaching. It ensures that learning experiences are equitable, proactive, and inclusive rather than reactive or remedial. Normalisation means that adjustments and choices—whether in content, process, or assessment—

are routine, visible, and expected for all students, removing any embarrassment or sense of difference.

When differentiation is the norm, students understand that everyone receives support tailored to their needs, and no one feels singled out for requiring "less" or "different" work. This practice builds a culture of respect, diversity, and confidence, where learners see their individual requirements as standard, not exceptional.

Normalising differentiation also involves regular review, collaboration with support networks, and fostering student agency. Planning is strengthened when teachers, students, and families work together to identify strengths, preferences, and goals without secrecy or shame.

Professional educators must lead the way, ensuring differentiation is embedded and celebrated, so that every learner feels their needs are an essential part of the classroom fabric, not an exception. In this way, we honour the diversity of minds and empower every student to succeed.

CHAPTER 16: HIGH-VOLTAGE HEARTS, HIGH-SPEED MINDS

Supporting Gifted Children in the Age of AI

"She used Gemini to research Roman architecture for fun. Then she built the Colosseum in Roblox."

Gifted children often experience the world in high definition—intellectually intense, emotionally deep, and relentlessly curious. Their minds don't idle. They soar, spiral, and question everything. But in traditional classrooms, these children can feel underwhelmed and unseen.

AI, when used with intention, can stretch their thinking, channel their passions, and soothe their perfectionism. And just as we saw in the chapter on learning differences, teachers often face an impossible task: meeting the needs of the child who is three steps ahead while also scaffolding the child still trying to take their first. AI is one way to hold those worlds together.

Ella's Story: The Midnight Meltdown

Ella was eleven, whip-smart, and a perfectionist. She loved writing stories and could spin entire worlds out of a single spark. But one Tuesday night, at 11:30pm, her mum found her at the desk in tears. The assignment — a persuasive essay on recycling — was already eight pages long. None of it, Ella sobbed, was "good enough."

Her mum tried to reassure her: "Sweetheart, your teacher only asked for two pages."

Ella pushed back: "But I can't stop. If it's not perfect, I don't know what it's missing."

The next day, Ella's teacher introduced her to an AI tool. Not to write for her, but to help her frame her ideas. Together they asked: "Check this essay like an English professor for a top student who wants explicit detailed feedback to ensure she gets full marks. Provide a checklist for self assessing." The AI produced a detailed checklist and identified two elements that were missing from her writing and even offered Ella suggestions that she hadn't thought of. For the first time, she knew when she was done. She finally stopped writing when she reached the target.

That night at home, her mum noticed something different. Ella printed her two-page essay and slid it into her folder with a quiet smile instead of tears. "I think it's enough," she whispered.

AI didn't shrink her brilliance. It gave her boundaries and an end point.

Parent's Voice

"I'm proud of her brilliance, but sometimes I feel like I'm holding a fire in my hands. She remembers everything, questions everything, feels everything. Dinner-table conversations become debates about ethics, climate change, or quantum physics. And yet, that same child will collapse in tears over a misspelled word.

I worry that I can't keep up—that I'm not enough to guide her. What if she grows restless? What if she burns out?

When she started using AI, something shifted. Suddenly, she had a companion who could match her questions at the speed they came, who didn't sigh or say 'maybe later.' She still needs me, but I no longer have to be her only sounding board. In that space, I can finally just be her parent again.

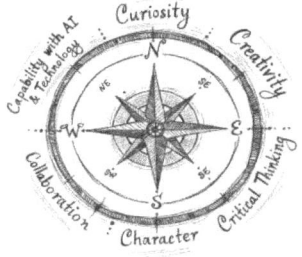

Jacob's Story: The Bored Boy Who Found His Stage

Jacob was fourteen and, according to his teachers, "coasting." He finished worksheets quickly and then stared out the window. When his parents asked him how school was, his answer was always the same, "Boring."

One afternoon his RE teacher noticed the slump in his shoulders and tried something different. "Jacob, how about you use Gemini to script a conversation between Aristotle and Elon Musk about the meaning of progress?"

Something lit up. That night, Jacob took it further — he asked the AI to help him design avatars, record the dialogue, and turn it into a short animated video. He showed his class the next day. They laughed in all the right places, debated his ideas, and asked him questions afterwards. For once, he wasn't invisible.

When his mum picked him up, he was animated in the car. "Mum, I think I might actually like philosophy. It's like… a game of ideas."

AI hadn't just stretched his intellect — it had given him a stage. For Jacob, who had spent years underchallenged and unseen, that stage felt like oxygen.

The Teacher Torn in Two

Parents aren't the only ones who feel this tension. Teachers are often split down the middle: some students can't yet form a sentence, while others are demanding more. The guilt of never giving enough to either side weighs heavily.

I felt it myself in one of the most difficult classes of my career. It was "camp chaos" — the widest range of learning needs I had ever taught. In the middle of it sat a girl with eyes that shone like her grandfather's.

That detail mattered. For seven years, I served as volunteer Medical Director for Ironman Australia. My husband and I coordinated more than 350 doctors, paramedics, nurses, medical students, and volunteers. One year, we were honoured with the Ironman Event of the Year. The head medical director — our close friend — entrusted me with another role years later, in the classroom. His son had been in my very first class, and I had watched his brilliance unfold into a career in medicine.

Now, more than a decade on, I was teaching his granddaughter.

Minutes into an activity, she looked up.

"Miss, what do I do now that I am finished?"

I froze for a moment. Around her, half the class hadn't even started. Do I extend her, or rescue them?

This is where AI became my co-teacher.

"Why don't you ask Gemini," I suggested, "to create a short presentation on why cherry blossoms are such a powerful symbol in Japanese culture—and how their meaning has changed over time."

Her eyes lit up. Within 20 minutes she had woven poetry, art, and modern tourism into slides, complete with AI-generated images of blossoms falling over Kyoto temples. She proudly presented to the class, elevating the room's energy.

For her, it wasn't "extra busy work." It was a doorway into wonder. For me, it was a relief. AI allowed me to sit shoulder-to-shoulder with struggling learners while ensuring she wasn't left idle or unseen.

What the Research Shows

- Dr. Susan Baum's work on twice-exceptional learners (2017) shows that giftedness combined with difference often leads to asynchronous development. AI can extend one area while scaffolding another.
- Dr. Linda Silverman highlights the power of technology-rich environments for visual-spatial learners—something AI can amplify through interactive prompts and simulations.
- Professor Tracy Riley found that digital enrichment boosts motivation, curiosity, and emotional regulation, especially for gifted students trapped in rigid curricula.

What You Can Do as a Parent

- Use AI as a launchpad: "What do you want to explore next?"

- Talk about process over perfection: "What did you learn from how you got there?"
- Encourage multimodal output: writing, designing, building, performing.
- Follow tangents: Gifted learners spiral intellectually; AI can help structure that spiral into something productive.

What Teachers Can Do

- Use AI to tier tasks: scaffolds for strugglers, extensions for sprinters.
- Set extension prompts are rooted in culture and creativity: "Compare haiku to sonnets," "Design a role-play of a tea ceremony," "Explore how anime reflects Japanese values."
- Let AI hold the "fast finishers" while you hold the fragile.

The Neurological Landscape of Giftedness: Understanding Cognitive and Emotional Complexity

The prevailing misconception that gifted children simply think faster fails to capture the profound neurological complexity underlying their cognitive architecture.

Contemporary neuroscience reveals that gifted learners' brains don't merely accelerate existing processes — they fundamentally restructure how information flows through neural networks, creating both remarkable capabilities and unique vulnerabilities.

Neuroimaging studies demonstrate that gifted children exhibit heightened amygdala activation, the brain's primary emotional processing centre, coupled with enhanced connectivity between the limbic system and prefrontal cortex (Piechowski, 2014). This neuroanatomical configuration produces what researchers term "emotional intensity"—a phenomenon where intellectual acceleration co-occurs with amplified emotional reactivity. Unlike neurotypical peers, gifted learners experience emotions with greater depth and duration, often struggling to regulate responses that feel disproportionate to triggering events.

The connectivity patterns extend beyond emotional processing. Advanced neuroimaging reveals that gifted individuals demonstrate extraordinary interconnectedness across divergent thinking networks—brain regions responsible for generating novel ideas and making unexpected connections. Simultaneously, their salience detection networks operate with hypervigilance, constantly scanning environments for subtle details and patterns that others overlook.

This neurological profile creates a paradox. The same neural architecture that enables creative breakthroughs and intellectual insights can overwhelm working memory systems. When divergent thinking networks and salience detection operate simultaneously at heightened levels, the resulting cognitive load can exceed processing capacity, triggering what appears as sudden emotional dysregulation.

This is where AI becomes a neurological ally in neurological learning and support. By allowing gifted learners to:

- Test ideas iteratively (without fear of judgement),
- Receive immediate, low-stakes feedback, and
- Externalise racing thoughts into structured prompts,

AI helps reduce what's known as cognitive-emotional load. When a child can "download" their intensity into dialogue with an AI, the prefrontal cortex (planning, reasoning) regains control over the limbic system (emotions), supporting emotional regulation.

When paired with reflective conversation—"How did that make you feel? What do you want to do next?" — AI isn't just a thinking partner. It becomes a neuroregulatory tool, calming the storm while still honouring the fire.

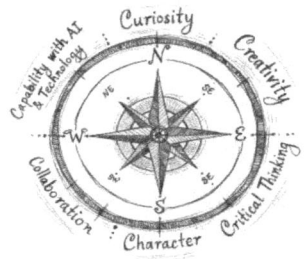

Classroom Example: The Brilliant but Fragile Year 8 Student

In my Year 8 Japanese class, there was one student whose brain worked like a spotlight. If I accidentally mis-wrote a kanji stroke, or if a grammar explanation had the slightest inconsistency, his hand would shoot up:

"Miss, isn't that particle actually marking direction, not time?"

He was right—often dazzlingly so. His questions were laser-sharp, logical, and far beyond what most 13-year-olds would think to ask. But with that brilliance came fragility.

One day, while practising a role-play ordering food in a restaurant, he stumbled over a line he had already mastered the week before. He froze, then his face crumpled.

"I can't do it. I'm hopeless," he whispered, pushing his script away. Later that week, when teams were picked for a group quiz, he wasn't chosen first. That too reduced him to quiet tears, followed by a shutdown where he refused to participate.

From a neuroscience perspective, this made sense: his prefrontal cortex (logic, planning) was overdeveloped for his age, but his limbic system (emotions) still responded with the rawness of a younger child. High intellect paired with high reactivity.

This was where AI became a stabiliser. Instead of leaving him trapped in shame after mistakes, I introduced him to Gemini for practice. He asked it to role-play as a "Japanese waiter" while he tried ordering meals. Each time he made an error, the AI simply corrected him without judgement, then repeated the line until he felt ready to move on.

Slowly, he started to reframe mistakes not as proof of failure, but as steps in iteration. Later, when he got stuck in class, I reminded him:

"Remember how the AI just waited for you last time? Let's try again. Mistakes are data, not disasters."

He smiled faintly and picked up his script again.

AI didn't erase his emotional intensity. It helped him carry it.

Teacher Reflection: What I Learned

As his teacher, I had to adjust my own expectations. At first, I thought extension alone would keep him satisfied — give him harder kanji, deeper grammar, and more complex tasks. But I realised quickly that intellectual challenge wasn't enough. His emotions could unravel faster than his brilliance could shine.

The biggest shift for me came when I stopped seeing his tears as weakness and started seeing them as a symptom of overload. He wasn't "overreacting" — his brain was simply processing at a higher pitch in both directions: more insight, more vulnerability.

AI became a bridge. It gave him a non-judgemental space to practise, to get things wrong safely, and to iterate until he felt mastery. That freedom allowed me to step back, to tend to the rest of the class, and then re-engage with him when he was calmer.

The lesson for me — and for any parent or teacher of a gifted child — is this. Giftedness is not just acceleration, it's amplification. The highs are higher, the lows are lower, and both need to be honoured. With the right scaffolds — human and technological — we can hold their brilliance without burning them out.

Parent Tip: Reducing the Sting of Mistakes at Home

For highly gifted children, getting something wrong can feel like humiliation — especially in public. Home can become a safe testing ground where mistakes lose their sting.

Try these prompts with your child:

- Invite exploration: Use AI to simulate a historical debate, co-write a story, or build a cultural project. These activities shift the focus from "getting it right" to discovery.
- Ask reflective questions: "What surprised you?" and "What's the next question you want to ask?" This reframes learning as an unfolding journey, not a pass/fail moment.
- Encourage teaching: Have them create content that teaches others what they've learned. Gifted learners thrive when they become guides — sharing knowledge builds confidence and resilience.

Remember: for gifted children, the key is to make mistakes private, safe, and productive before they're asked to step onto a public stage.

Final Thought

Gifted learners don't break neatly into boxes — they blaze, stumble, question, and feel with an intensity that can both inspire and exhaust. They don't need extra piles of worksheets. They need wonder, challenge, and the safety to fall apart and try again.

Parents, teachers, and mentors are the steady hands that hold both their brilliance and their fragility. AI, when used wisely, doesn't dim their light or tame their fire. It offers a safe place to test, to iterate, to dream aloud — so their intensity is not a burden but a gift.

Because these children don't just work a little faster in this world. They're here to help reimagine it.

PART FIVE: TAKING ACTION

CHAPTER 17: EMPOWERING YOUR HOME WITH AI

Welcome to the practical chapter — the one where vision meets action. You don't need to be a tech expert to build an AI-empowered home. What matters most is curiosity, intention, and a willingness to grow alongside your child. AI in the home isn't just about apps or smart speakers — it's about creating an environment where learning, questioning, and creative thinking are part of daily life.

Setting Up Your Family AI Toolkit

Start small with low-stakes, high-impact tools:

- AI Chat Assistants (Perplexity, Gemini, Claude): Use for homework help, brainstorming, writing outlines, or summarising articles.

- Voice-to-Text Tools: Ideal for children who struggle with writing but have strong verbal reasoning. Voice typing helps children with dyslexia or motor coordination difficulties express themselves.
- Visual Generators (Canva AI, DALL·E, Adobe Firefly): Great for storytelling, illustrating projects, or designing digital art.
- Organisation Helpers (Goblin Tools, Todoist): Break tasks into steps or build routines to support executive functioning.

Create a "Digital Discovery Station" at home — one place (physical or virtual) where AI tools are bookmarked and ready. When questions come up like "Can you explain this like I'm 10?" or "Help me create a quiz for science," the tools are there, easy to use, and stress-free.

Start small. Use AI for everyday fun. By lowering the stakes, you reduce pressure and build confidence.

Family Culture Shift

Building an AI-literate home is more about values than tools. In early childhood education, educators often refer to the environment as the "Third Teacher" — the space around us shapes how children think and feel.

In an AI-powered world, this becomes even more critical. When we place books and devices side by side, prompts on the wall, and creativity tools within reach, we send a clear message: this is a home where questions matter, where curiosity is celebrated, where learning is safe and dynamic.

Some practical shifts:

- Celebrate questions, not just answers. Use AI as a launchpad for deeper conversations, not an endpoint.
- Encourage
- Rotate leadership. Let children teach parents how to use AI. Co-learning builds confidence and equality.

- Model ethical use. Say out loud: "Where did this information come from?" or "How can I fact check this?"
- Avoid fear-based messaging. Instead of "AI is dangerous," try "AI is powerful — and it's our job to use it wisely."
- Make AI shared, not secret. Frame it as a family tool, not a forbidden shortcut.

Home AI Use Agreement

Create a family agreement to make boundaries clear:

- When it's okay to use AI (not during assessments or without teacher permission).
- What kind of help is allowed (brainstorming vs. final drafts).
- Ethical guardrails (fact-checking, citing sources).
- Who to talk to when unsure (parent, teacher, mentor).
- Display it in your digital workspace. Revisit it each term or year as your child matures.

- Use AI to expand thinking, deepen learning and understanding not simply to take short cut or

Real-World Family Examples

Here are some of the ways families (including mine) are using AI right now — across everyday life, special events, and even deeply personal moments.

Money Savers

- Scan weekly supermarket specials and create five family-friendly meals under $20 (with dietary needs).
- Upload recent grocery receipts and ask AI for cost-cutting strategies to reduce the weekly shop.
- Take a photo of the contents of the fridge and create 3 meals from existing items.
- Use AI to compare phone, internet, or utility plans and show pros and cons in plain English.
- Have AI analyse household habits and energy bills then give appliance by appliance savings, off-peak usage adjustments, top power drainers, small changes that save big.

- What to buy and when alerts. Ask AI to scan for historically low times of the year to buy big tickets or regular items.
- As a DIY fix it guide or IT help support. Ask AI to provide step by step guides for many problems that can be solved before a service call.
- AI Sports and Hobby Savings Planner. Enter sports, term fees, uniform costs, competition travel and accommodation along with equipment needs to give a full year forecast and money-saving alternatives for second hand gear, club swaps and best times to buy.
- Upload photos of items to be sold online on marketplace and have AI generate a post and recommended sale price for quick sale.
- Car repair/parts. Before paying for work, paste a mechanical quote and ask AI what is essential, what can wait, what are cheaper alternatives, what are the typical price ranges.
- Use AI to size-check clothing across brands by entering body proportions + favourite labels to

remove the frustration of online shopping and to find cheaper alternatives.

Family Fun & Everyday Helpers

- Design a family chores roster that is equitable. Include time allocations and ask AI for (non-monetry) rewards.
- Create bedtime stories where the child is the main character and the family pet becomes the hero.
- Ask AI to design fitness plans for everyone: mum's gym training, dad's ski season prep, and kids' new basketball plays—all in one shared half-hour.
- Generate birthday party themes with menus, treasure hunts, printable invites, and playlists.
- Use AI as a family mediator: enter both sides of a disagreement (e.g., screen time vs. homework) and get compromise options to discuss calmly.
- Chef Roulette. Each family member chooses one ingredient and AI turns all random ingredients

into a single recipe. Kids love seeing what meals come out of the AI dinner challenge.
- Sibling Conflict Mediator. Parents type in both sides of an argument. AI gives non-biased fair, calm solutions that feel neutral and rebuild connection. Kids feel respected, not lectured.
- Dinner Table Topics. AI generates fun, silly, deep or meaningful prompts. Families report better conversations and less screen distraction at dinner.

Holidays & Celebrations

- Plan Christmas from start to finish: gift lists by age and budget, stocking fillers, allergy-friendly menus, ensuring that stockings are equitable.
- Turn family photos into AI-designed memory books or slideshows for grandparents.
- Use AI to create time capsule letters for the family to read in 10 years.
- Custom Holiday Planner. Build a fully customised itinerary incorporating each family

member's preferences for activities, food stops, hidden gems, weather-safe alternatives and transports. Ensure that you outline what your previous favourite holiday consisted of to ensure alignment.
- Family Traditions Designer. Create brand-new traditions based on culture, values and quirks. Kids adore traditions that feel uniquely theirs.
- Celebration Speechwriter. AI can help you write something heartfelt, funny, or moving that is deeply personalised.

Big Events

- For a wedding, ask AI to generate three different versions of the day—luxury, budget, and minimalist—then compare menus, venues, guest lists, and playlists side by side.
- Create speech drafts for birthdays, retirements, or farewells, blending humour and heart. Wedding vows, funeral readings, birth announcements, legacy letters

- Work with different family members to write a eulogy together: each person can share memories, AI helps with flow, and the result is a voice that truly represents everyone.
- Event Planner and Timeline Builder. AI creates full run sheets for all major events that includes, timing, cues, seating arrangements, music suggestions, and contingency plans, reducing stress so people can be present, relaxed and enjoy the time with family and friends.
- Translation for multilingual ceremonies.
- Cultural inclusivity to major celebrations to ensure that all guests feel respected and deeply connected.
- Pronunciation assistance for family names and places.

Emotional Intelligence in the AI Age

In an AI-powered home, emotional intelligence matters more than ever. Tools can give your child answers. Only relationships can help them grow in character.

Encourage:

- Empathy: Talk about how AI should be used to uplift, not deceive.
- Self-awareness: Ask, "How did that tool make you feel?" or "Were you proud of that work?"
- Perspective-taking: Explore bias in AI responses. Ask, "Why might it answer differently for one person than another?"

Digital Wellbeing and Boundaries

AI can be captivating, but families need rhythms of rest.

- Create tech-off rituals (devices down after 8pm, AI-free Sundays).
- Teach children to notice when curiosity tips into fatigue.
- Use AI to support balance: "Make me a 5-minute bedtime wind-down plan."

AI for Family Connection

AI doesn't need to be solo. It can strengthen family rituals:

- Generate weekly meal plans together.
- Make a family trivia quiz on history, culture, or faith.
- Design holiday itineraries or themed parties with children leading.
- Write bedtime stories together ("Make the dog the hero!").

When children become the teacher—showing parents how to use tools—they grow in confidence and you model shared learning.

Future-Proof Skills at Home

We can't predict the exact jobs our children will one day have, but we do know the skills they'll need to thrive in any future. These six—critical thinking, creativity, collaboration, adaptability, ethical reasoning, and communication—are flexible, transferable and timeless.

At home, you can nurture critical thinking by encouraging your child to question and compare what AI gives them. Ask a question, then fact-check the response in a book or reliable website. At the dinner table, compare two AI answers and invite them to decide which is more accurate and why. Help them notice not just what was said, but what was missing. Interestingly, gaming often builds similar skills. A child who learns to analyse an opponent's strategy in a multiplayer game is also sharpening their ability to weigh options and make logical judgements in real life.

Creativity can be sparked by co-writing stories with AI, but letting your child choose the twists and turns. Use AI art tools to design postcards or birthday cards, then challenge them with questions such as: "How would you make this idea even better?" When AI becomes a springboard rather than the final product, children discover the joy of building on ideas, not just receiving them.

For collaboration, make AI a family activity. Plan a holiday together—one person researching activities, another checking costs, another creating the itinerary. Or brainstorm a family project and divide tasks, with everyone contributing to the prompt before asking AI to bring it together. These small projects mirror the teamwork skills that will define their adult lives.

Adaptability is about learning to adjust when things don't go to plan. When AI gets an answer wrong, resist the urge to discard it; instead, show your child how to reframe the question: "How else can we ask this?" Revert to the CLARITY model of prompting. Experiment with different tools and talk about how their outputs differ. Praise them not only for the "right" answer, but for the flexibility they showed in trying again or trying from a different angle.

Ethical reasoning can grow from simple conversations. Debate dilemmas as a family: "Should AI grade essays?" or "Should robots care for the elderly?" Model integrity by citing AI outputs, checking sources, and talking openly about bias. Ask questions such as: "Where did this answer come from? Should we trust it?" These habits train children to carry their values into an automated world.

Finally, strong communication ensures they can share their ideas with clarity and empathy. Ask your child to "teach back" what AI explained in their own words. Use voice-to-text to practise oral explanations, or challenge them to simplify a concept: "Explain this as if you were talking to a six-year-old." Each of these practices strengthens not just knowledge, but the ability to connect that knowledge to others.

These aren't school skills—they are life skills. And just like literacy or numeracy, they will serve your child no matter what the future holds. By weaving them into everyday family life, you prepare your child not just for exams or university, but for a world that rewards thinkers, makers, and collaborators above all.

Creating a Resilient AI Home Environment

Gifted or not, children need resilience, and AI can become a useful partner in building it. Start by normalising mistakes—laugh together when AI "gets it wrong" and treat errors as opportunities rather than failures. Encourage persistence by prompting your child to try again with a new question instead of giving up at the first hurdle. Alongside this, emphasize the importance of protecting their identity, making it clear that personal details should never be shared with AI tools. Finally, frame AI as a form of literacy, just like reading or maths—something that takes time, practice, and patience to master, but that will remain a valuable lifelong skill.

For example, one parent described how their child grew frustrated when AI gave confusing answers to a science question. Instead of letting the frustration escalate, they encouraged their child to rephrase the question, try a different tool, and compare the outputs. Over time, the child began to see that the "failure" wasn't theirs—it was part of the process. Much like retrying a level in a video game or rewriting a paragraph in an essay, each attempt was simply another path forward. In this way, resilience wasn't taught as an abstract value, but as a lived experience of turning setbacks into strategies.

A Long-Term View

The goal isn't instant mastery — it's gradual fluency. What matters isn't how quickly your child learns to prompt but how wisely they learn to question and interpret.

Let your home be the place where new ideas are tested, mistakes are safe, and creativity is nurtured. You don't need to predict your child's career. You just need to build the skills that outlast every job.

Critical Thinking

- ☐ Use AI to Compare, Contrast, and Challegen Ideas (The Triangulation Method) Ask AI a question, then double-check in a book or site.

- ☐ Compare two AI answers: "Which is more accurate? Why?"

- ☐ Ask: "What's missing here?"

- ☐ Instead of using one prompt, build a series of prompts:

- Explain this concept in simple terms appropriate for a (X) year old.
- Challenge this explanation from an opposition's perspective.
- Give me an analogy.
- Show me the limitations, identify risks I haven't considered.
- What is overgeneralised, vague, unsupported or assumed?

By developing these critical thinking skills students are encouraged to deepen their thinking and promote metacognition. By asking AI to play devil's advocate it encourages students to shift AI away from an 'answer machine' to a 'thinking partner', thus developing cognitive flexibility, sophisticated reasoning and ultimately is an essential reflective practice in an AI dominated world.

Creativity

☐ Co-write a silly story with AI. Write one sentence each

☐ Design fictional societies, ecosystems, companies, or historical what-ifs, using AI to test ideas, fill gaps, or simulate consequences. This blends imagination with systems thinking.

☐ Ask: "How can you improve this?"

☐ Ask AI for multiple creative variations of the same idea - different tones, perspectives, settings, genres or artistic interpretations then analyze which version is the most original and why.

☐ Ask AI to set unusual constraints (eg "Write a story with no adjectives" or "Solve this problem using only analogies"). Creative constraints trigger flexible, non-linear thinking.

Collaboration

☐ Rotating roles in group tasks: prompt engineer, evidence checker, synthesiser, presenter.

☐ Brainstorm a project together. Ideas must be debated, justified and then the best idea is selected. It forces negotiation, consensus building and shared decision making.

- [ ] Try: "We each add one detail to the prompt."
- [ ] AI mediated conflict resolution.
- [ ] Group debate with AI as the opposition.
- [ ] Collaborative text-building. Each member of the group contributes one section of a shared document and AI provides real-time cohesion and transitions.

Adaptability

- [ ] Reframe when AI is wrong: "How else could we ask?"
- [ ] Compare two AI tools.
- [ ] Praise flexible thinking.
- [ ] Change one variable of a task (time period, constraints, materials, audience). They must adapt their thinking accordingly.

- ☐ AI-simulated unexpected problem. Ask AI to introduce hurdles into a project (limit budget, new rule, stakeholder shift). Students must redesign their plan.

- ☐ Students ask for alternate interpretations of the same situation, historical, scientific, emotional, ethical. They practise flexible perspective-taking.

- ☐ Scenario swapping. Ask AI to generate scenarios with peers and adapt their prior plan to a new context.

Ethical Reasoning

- ☐ Debate dilemmas (AI grading essays, robots as carers).

- ☐ Bias-spotting challenges. Students ask AI to analyse controversial topics then examine its potential biases, omissions or flawed reasoning.

- ☐ Ask AI to verify claims, identify misinformation and justify which sources should be trusted.

- ☐ Digital Footprint Simulations. AI shows possible consequences of online decisions (eg: oversharing, cyberbullying). Students discuss responsibility, privacy and impact.

Communication

☐ Have your child teach back an AI answer.

☐ Practise explaining with voice-to-text.

☐ Ask: "Explain this to a 6-year-old." "What part of my message is unclear?"

☐ Have AI rewrite their message in tones such as professional, empathetic, assertive, persuasive. They learn stylistic precision.

☐ Have students rewrite content for multiple audiences, parents, peers, experts, early learners. This teaches adaptability and communication.

☐ Role-play conversations (interviewers, customers, historical figures).

Parent Tip: Pick just one or two skills each week. Small habits grow strong roots.

These six capabilities — critical thinking, creativity, collaboration, communication, adaptability, and ethical reasoning — are the real future-proof skills our children need. AI can strengthen each of them when used deliberately in the classroom: helping students analyse ideas more deeply, generate original thinking, work together more effectively, express themselves with clarity, pivot when situations change, and make decisions grounded in values rather than convenience. The truth is, we don't know what jobs will exist in ten years (let alone two years!). We don't know which industries will rise or fall, or which technologies will reshape our world next. But we do know this: young people who can think well, create boldly, collaborate wisely, adapt quickly, communicate clearly, and act ethically will thrive in any future we step into. These skills are not optional anymore — they are the foundation on which every unknown opportunity will be built.

Final Thought

Your home doesn't need the latest gadgets or perfect systems to prepare your child for the future. What it needs is trust, conversation, and curiosity. When you invite AI into family life with intention, you're not raising a child to master a machine—you're raising a child to master themselves: to think critically, create boldly, adapt gracefully, and lead with empathy.

In the end, AI is just a tool. The real power is in the values you model, the questions you ask, and the courage you show in learning alongside your child. That's what future-proofs them—not knowing every answer, but knowing how to ask, how to grow, and how to walk into an unknown world with confidence and hope.

CHAPTER 18: NAVIGATING THE FUTURE TOGETHER

The future isn't something your child will walk into alone. It's something you will step into together.

As AI reshapes education, work, and creativity, your role as a parent is not to know everything but to stay present, curious, and open. You don't need to master every new tool. What matters most is that you keep showing up.

Parenting with a compass, not a map

No parent has the full map of where this is heading. Technology shifts faster than schools, policies, or workplaces can keep up. That's daunting. But it also means we can stop chasing the illusion of certainty.

What you can give your child:

- Ethics — knowing how to use power wisely.
- Empathy — staying human in the face of automation.
- Creativity — seeing possibilities others might miss.
- Critical thinking — asking: Is this true? Is this good? What are the consequences?
- Resilience — reframing mistakes as part of growth, not humiliation.
- Collaboration — recognising that in tomorrow's world, no one builds alone.

These are the survival skills of the AI era. They cannot be downloaded. They cannot be automated. They are lived and modelled—and you are the model.

The Dinner Table Advantage

One of the most underrated tools in your home is the dinner table. You don't need a program, a textbook, or a polished plan—you simply need presence. Use this time to ask questions such as, "What did you use AI for today?" or "Did you agree with what it gave you? Why or why not?" You might even stretch their imagination with, "If a robot became your school principal, how would things change?"

These conversations do more than pass the salt. They give your child practice in reasoning, reflection, and debate, while sending a clear message that curiosity is valued. In a world obsessed with speed, the slow ritual of conversation is nothing short of revolutionary.

I saw this come to life when I shared a recent headline with my son: the Polish rum company Dictador has appointed a robotic AI, Mika, as its CEO. Instead of brushing past it, I asked, "What do you think would happen if your school had an AI principal alongside the human one? Would it be fairer? Stricter? More creative?" That simple question unlocked a conversation about leadership, trust, and the limits of machines. He wondered if an AI principal might reduce favouritism but also worried it might not understand emotions or context.

Within minutes, we were talking about bias, ethics, and the importance of keeping people in the loop.

That's the power of a good question: it transforms technology from something distant and abstract into a springboard for family dialogue about values, fairness, and the kind of future we want to build together.

From Consumers to Creators

One of the greatest risks of AI is that children become passive—consuming outputs rather than shaping them. But we need to pause here and notice something important. We call it generative AI because it generates new ideas, images, or texts from what it has been trained on. Yet isn't this exactly what we ask our students to do in school? We want them to generate essays from research, solutions from formulas, insights from history, or creative products from inspiration. In a sense, AI is simply reflecting back the very same generative process we have always valued in human learning.

The difference is that children cannot compete with AI on memory or speed—and they shouldn't have to.

Machines do that well. What children need is to evolve beyond the old measures of success. They need to create content that carries their unique perspective, critique information with discernment, and collaborate with others to build something AI alone could never achieve.

You can help them practise this shift at home by asking them to push beyond what AI gives them. Try questions like: "How can you make this more creative?" or "What would you add that AI couldn't possibly know?" or "Could you turn this into something you could teach a younger sibling?"

When children move from consumers to creators, from passive receivers to active shapers, they stop being swept along by technology and start steering it. And in that evolution, they discover the skill that AI can never replicate: the ability to make meaning, not just content.

Gaming, AI and the Skills That Last

AI is not going away. And neither is gaming. These are the worlds our children are growing up in. The question is not whether they should use them, but how we guide them to use them well. Parents often see gaming as a waste of time, yet beneath the surface, games are developing skills that matter far beyond the screen. Strategic thinking in planning a move mirrors the planning needed for projects in work and life. The resilience required to keep trying after losing a round is the same resilience needed after setbacks in studies or careers. Collaboration in co-operative missions reflects the teamwork essential in workplaces. Adaptability in facing new game levels is not so different from navigating career changes. Even the ability to stay focused under pressure in a timed battle is the same skill that helps manage deadlines calmly.

AI develops parallel strengths. Asking children to check whether an answer is accurate builds critical thinking. Co-writing a story, designing an image, or solving a problem together nurtures creativity. Using AI with peers or family members mirrors collaboration. Debating whether an AI response is fair or biased strengthens ethical reasoning. And having a child explain back what

AI produced, or simplify it for a younger sibling, sharpens communication.

The real task for parents is to help children make the link. What looks like play or quick answers can be reframed as skill-building. A simple observation such as, "What you're doing in this game is teamwork under pressure—that's a skill you'll need anywhere," or, "AI just gave you three answers—how will you decide which is the best one?" turns passive activity into reflective practice. When children connect what they are doing in games or with AI to real-world application, the shift happens: from entertainment to education, from distraction to development.

And when we step back, the picture becomes clear. AI isn't going away. Gaming isn't going away. The future belongs to those who can navigate both with wisdom. The people who will thrive in the future won't be the ones who embrace AI the fastest, but the ones who learn to navigate it the widest, exploring its limits, its possibilities, and its full potential with curiosity and confidence. The skills that matter most — critical thinking, creativity, collaboration, adaptability, ethical reasoning, communication, resilience, and empathy — are not optional extras. They are the new core curriculum of life in an AI-driven world. These are the abilities that will carry our children forward, no matter what job titles or industries exist in the decades ahead.

Co-Education Is the New Education

Schools cannot do this work alone, and neither can families. The strongest future lies in partnership.

If we recall the teacher who built an AI chatbot for his Economics students at HSC level. No single teacher could ever have provided that level of support. Their results soared — but what they valued most wasn't the bot itself. It was that in class, they still had a teacher who saw them, guided them, and believed in them.

That's the lesson for parents too. AI can supplement, but it cannot substitute. The human connection still matters most.

Education in this new era isn't about handing learning entirely to schools or entirely to families. It's about co-education: homes and schools working together to create safe, flexible pathways that value wellbeing as much as achievement.

What Parents Really Need to Hear

You may feel behind. You may worry that your child knows more than you, that the world is moving too fast, that you can't keep up. That's okay.

Your child does not need you to have every answer.

What they need is you.

- Your wisdom.
- Your curiosity.
- Your presence.

AI can give them knowledge. You can give them grounding.

AI can spark ideas. You can give them values.

AI can offer feedback. You can give them love.

That combination—the best of both worlds—is what will future-proof them.

The Brain Is Built for Change

From a neuroscience perspective, Darren explains that the brain is wired for change. Neuroplasticity—a term we introduced in Chapter One—describes how the brain learns by growing new pathways and strengthening existing connections. It is not a static organ but a dynamic, living system, constantly reshaping itself in response to challenge, emotion, and experience.

Every time a child engages in new, difficult, and emotionally meaningful learning, they are literally rewiring their brain. This is neuroplasticity in action—not an abstract theory, but a biological reality happening in classrooms, homes, and playgrounds every day.

Artificial intelligence, when used well, can accelerate that process. It can scaffold memory, provide immediate feedback, and simulate complex problem-solving environments. But this acceleration comes with a caveat: it must be anchored in ethics, creativity, empathy, and critical thought. Without those anchors, we risk producing efficiency without wisdom, or speed without depth.

As one parent recently said with such honesty and relief, "I finally understand that AI isn't a shortcut. It's not going to make my son lazy. When used well with the right guidance and guard rails it can be a tutor, a thinking partner, a collaborator. It's neutral until we teach our children how to use it. Now I can see that AI isn't replacing learning at all. It is deepening it and it's simply becoming part of how our kids learn moving forward.

This is both a reminder and a challenge. It signals the future of education—adaptive to individual learners, ethical in its design, and profoundly human in its purpose. The task before us is not to resist AI, but to shape it in service of what makes us most human: our ability to learn, to connect, and to grow.

A Legacy of Hope

As parents, you are not on the sidelines. You are right in the middle of this unfolding story — walking beside your child into tomorrow.

Let that be your family's legacy: not fear, not fatigue, but readiness, resilience, and hope.

Your children won't remember every app or device. What they will remember is that when the world shifted, you didn't panic. You stayed curious. You asked questions. You modelled how to navigate change.

The future doesn't belong to those who memorise the most. It belongs to those who can collaborate, create, and think critically with compassion.

And the good news is this: you don't have to do it perfectly. You just have to do it together.

Walking Into Tomorrow

For years, I never really understood my eldest son's love of gaming. To be honest, I worried about it. The hours spent in front of a screen. The language I didn't recognise. The passion for a world I wasn't part of. We didn't encourage it, we actively pushed against it. But lately, I've started to see something I can't ignore: management qualities emerging from him that I know we haven't taught him. The way he organises a team of players across multiple time zones. The strategies he uses to rally others when a game turns difficult. The persistence he shows after setbacks, leading rather than withdrawing.

It's not the path I would have chosen for him. But it's a path that's teaching him skills We recognise: leadership, collaboration, adaptability under pressure. Skills that will matter just as much in boardrooms, hospitals, classrooms, and businesses as they do in a digital world.

That's when it struck me: the future won't look like the past. Our children's classrooms are bigger than the ones we sat in, and their teachers are not always the adults standing at the front of a room. Gaming, AI, technology — these are not distractions to be feared, but arenas where skills are forged.

And as parents, we don't need to understand every detail to walk alongside them. We just need to notice, to ask, to connect the dots: "What you're learning here can take you anywhere."

That is what navigating the future together looks like. Not control. Not fear. But presence. The courage to admit we don't always get it, and the humility to learn what our children are already teaching us.

Conclusion – Raising Adaptable Learners in an Age of Acceleration

We're no longer preparing our children for a future — we are parenting in it so that our children can be confident active participants in shaping the future. Artificial intelligence, once an abstract concept, is now part of our children's classrooms, conversations, and creative processes. For many parents, this shift feels disorienting. We didn't grow up with AI as a study buddy, or with algorithms nudging our choices. So how do we help our children grow up well, in a world moving this fast?

Here's what we do:

We stop trying to prepare them for a fixed path. And instead, we raise them to adapt—with empathy, courage, and curiosity.

What Can Parents Do?

Children look to us not just for answers, but for how we respond to the unknown. They mirror our mindset. So we must show them that we are learning too.

To foster adaptability and navigate new learning models:

- Model a learning mindset: Let your children see you wrestle with unfamiliar technology or admit

when you don't know something — then learn it alongside them.
- Encourage "What if?" conversations: Prompt imagination, not just instruction. Ask questions that let your child dream, explore, and predict.
- Celebrate process over perfection: Praise how your child thinks, not just what they produce. This builds resilience.
- Empower prompt literacy and fluency: Collaborate to develop effective AI prompts and reflect on the quality of the responses.

How Do We Balance Technology?

- The goal is not to eliminate screen time — but to elevate it.
- To balance tech use without overwhelming children:
- Curate before you regulate: Choose tools that support creative expression, personalised learning, or emotional growth.

- Create tech rhythms: Instead of rules that punish, set routines that guide—like "Tech-free Thursdays" or "Screen Sundays with purpose."
- Co-explore: Watch your child use AI, ask them to explain how it works, and learn together. Shared learning reduces isolation and builds trust.
- Notice emotional cues: If your child seems more anxious, irritable, or distracted after using tech, use that as a discussion starter.

What Is the School's Role?

- Schools must be more than content factories. They need to become adaptive ecosystems that honour the individuality of every learner.
- Schools can support parental involvement by:
- Opening the AI conversation: Hosting family nights, guides, or digital portals to explain how AI is used in class.
- Offering training and tools: Helping parents understand how to support digital literacy and ethical tech use at home.

- Listening to families: Creating feedback loops that go beyond academic results to include emotional wellbeing and tech confidence.
- Partnering on future skills: Empowering parents to reinforce skills like critical thinking, creativity, and communication.
- When schools and families align — not in control, but in curiosity — students thrive.

One of the most important responsibilities schools now hold is investing in meaningful professional development for teachers in the use of AI. Our educators need support, time, and confidence to walk this journey alongside their students. Without this, young people will simply bumble their way through on their own — using AI inconsistently, without the ethical grounding, critical questioning, or understanding that safe use requires. Many teachers are already saving hours with AI, but these hours cannot just disappear into workload relief; they must be reinvested into learning how to use AI well, how to teach with it effectively, and how to guide students in using these tools with integrity. If we want students to use AI thoughtfully, safely, and with purpose, then teachers must be empowered first.

BIBLIOGRAPHY

PART ONE: OVERWHELMED

Chapter 1: The Truth About Modern Learning

Chan, K. S., & Zary, N. (2019). Applications and challenges of implementing artificial intelligence in medical education: integrative review. JMIR medical education, 5(1), e13930.
https://doi.org/10.2196/13930

Stošić, L., & Janković, A. (2023). The impact of artificial intelligence (AI) on education: Balancing advancements and ethical considerations on human rights. Pravo - teorija i praksa.
https://www.ceeol.com/search/article-detail?id=1213032

Holmes, W., Bialik, M., & Fadel, C. (2019). Artificial intelligence in education: Promises and implications for teaching and learning. Center for Curriculum Redesign. https://curriculumredesign.org/wp-content/uploads/AIED-Book-Excerpt-CCR.pdf

Hwang, G. J., & Chang, C. Y. (2023). A review of opportunities and challenges of chatbots in education. Interactive Learning Environments, 31(7), 4099-4112.
https://doi.org/10.1080/10494820.2021.1952615

Luckin, R., Holmes, W., Griffiths, M., & Forcier, L. B. (2016). Intelligence Unleashed: An Argument for AI in Education. Pearson.
https://static.googleusercontent.com/media/edu.google.com/en//pds/Intelligence-Unleashed-Publication.pdf

Popenici, S. A., & Kerr, S. (2017). Exploring the impact of artificial intelligence on teaching and learning in higher education. Research and practice in technology enhanced learning, 12(1), 22. https://doi.org/10.1186/s41039-017-0062-8

Prensky, M. (2001). Digital natives, digital immigrants part 1. On the Horizon, 9(5), 1-6. https://desarrollodocente.uc.cl/wp-content/uploads/2020/03/Digital_Natives_Digital_Inmigrants.pdf

Roll, I., & Wylie, R. (2016). Evolution and revolution in artificial intelligence in education. International journal of artificial intelligence in education, 26(2), 582-599.
https://doi.org/10.1007/s40593-016-0110-3

Sharples, M. (2019). Practical pedagogy: 40 new ways to teach and learn. Routledge. https://doi.org/10.4324/9780429485534

Zawacki-Richter, O., Marín, V. I., Bond, M., & Gouverneur, F. (2019). Systematic review of research on artificial intelligence applications in higher education–where are the educators?. International journal of educational technology in higher education, 16(1), 1-27. https://doi.org/10.1186/s41239-019-0171-0

Chapter 2: Gamer Minds – Turning Play into Purpose

All, A., Castellar, E. P. N., & Van Looy, J. (2016). Assessing the effectiveness of digital game-based learning: Best practices. Computers & Education, 92, 90-103.
https://doi.org/10.1016/j.compedu.2015.10.007

Bavelier, D., Green, C. S., Pouget, A., & Schrater, P. (2012). Brain plasticity through the life span: learning to learn and action video games. Annual review of neuroscience, 35, 391-416.
https://doi.org/10.1146/annurev-neuro-060909-152832

Carter, M., Moore, K., Mavoa, J., Gaspard, L., & Horst, H. (2020). Children's perspectives and attitudes towards Fortnite 'addiction'.

Media International Australia, 176(1), 138-151. https://doi.org/10.1177/1329878X20921568

Carter, M., Moore, K., Mavoa, J., Horst, H., & Gaspard, L. (2020). Situating the appeal of Fortnite within children's changing play cultures. Games and Culture, 15(4), 453-471. https://doi.org/10.1177/1555412020913771

Rideout, V., Peebles, A., Mann, S., & Robb, M. B. (2022). Common Sense census: Media use by tweens and teens, 2021. Common Sense. https://www.commonsensemedia.org/sites/default/files/research/report/8-18-census-integrated-report-final-web_0.pdf

Cowan, K., Potter, J., Olusoga, Y., Bannister, C., Bishop, J. C., Cannon, M., & Signorelli, V. (2021). Children's digital play during the COVID-19 pandemic: Insights from the play observatory. Je-LKS: Journal of e-Learning and Knowledge Society, 17(3), 8-17. https://doi.org/10.20368/1971-8829/1135590

Coyne, S. M., Jensen, A. C., Smith, N. J., & Erickson, D. H. (2016). Super Mario brothers and sisters: Associations between coplaying video games and sibling conflict and affection. Journal of adolescence, 47, 48-59. https://doi.org/10.1016/j.adolescence.2015.12.001

Dye, M. W., Green, C. S., & Bavelier, D. (2009). Increasing speed of processing with action video games. Current directions in psychological science, 18(6), 321-326. https://doi.org/10.1111/j.1467-8721.2009.01660.x

National Poll on Children's Health. (2020). Game on: Teens and video games (Vol. 35, Issue 4). C.S. Mott Children's Hospital. https://mottpoll.org/reports/game-teens-and-video-games

Gao, Y. X., Wang, J. Y., & Dong, G. H. (2022). The prevalence and possible risk factors of internet gaming disorder among adolescents and young adults: Systematic reviews and meta-analyses. Journal of psychiatric research, 154, 35-43.
https://doi.org/10.1016/j.jpsychires.2022.06.049

Gee, J. P. (2013). The anti-education era: creating smarter students through digital learning. Palgrave Macmillan. https://cmc.marmot.org/Record/.b37707577

Granic, I., Lobel, A., & Engels, R. C. (2014). The benefits of playing video games. American psychologist, 69(1), 66–78.
https://doi.org/10.1037/a0034857

Jackson, L. A., Witt, E. A., Games, A. I., Fitzgerald, H. E., Von Eye, A., & Zhao, Y. (2012). Information technology use and creativity: Findings from the Children and Technology Project. Computers in human behavior, 28(2), 370-376.
https://doi.org/10.1016/j.chb.2011.10.006

Kahila, J., Tedre, M., Kahila, S., Vartiainen, H., Valtonen, T., & Mäkitalo, K. (2021). Children's gaming involves much more than the gaming itself: A study of the metagame among 12-to 15-year-old children. Convergence, 27(3), 768-786.
https://doi.org/10.1177/1354856520979482

Ke, F. (2016). Designing and integrating purposeful learning in game play: A systematic review. Educational Technology Research and Development, 64(2), 219-244.
https://doi.org/10.1007/s11423-015-9418-1

Kutner, L. A., Olson, C. K., Warner, D. E., & Hertzog, S. M. (2008). Parents' and sons' perspectives on video game play: A qualitative study. Journal of Adolescent Research, 23(1), 76-96.
https://doi.org/10.1177/0743558407310721

Livingstone, S., & Pothong, K. (2021). Playful by design: Free play in a digital world. 5Rights Foundation. https://eprints.lse.ac.uk/119740/

Mavoa, J., Carter, M., & Gibbs, M. (2017). Children and Minecraft: A survey of children's digital play. New Media & Society, 20(9), 3283-3303. https://doi.org/10.1177/1461444817745320

Mazurek, M. O., & Engelhardt, C. R. (2013). Video game use in boys with autism spectrum disorder, ADHD, or typical development. Pediatrics, 132(2), 260-266. https://doi.org/10.1542/peds.2012-3956

McClain, C. (2022). How parents' views of their kids' screen time, social media use changed during COVID-19. Pew research center. https://coilink.org/20.500.12592/jj4b3z

Musick, G., Freeman, G., & McNeese, N. J. (2021). Gaming as family time: Digital game co-play in modern parent-child relationships. Proceedings of the ACM on Human-Computer Interaction, 5(CHI PLAY), 1-25. https://doi.org/10.1145/3474678

Navarro, J. (2020). Fortnite: a context for child development in the U.S. during COVID-19 (and beyond). Journal of Children and Media, 15(1), 13–16. https://doi.org/10.1080/17482798.2020.1858435

Pearce, K. E., Yip, J. C., Lee, J. H., Martinez, J. J., Windleharth, T. W., Bhattacharya, A., & Li, Q. (2022). Families playing animal crossing together: coping with video games during the COVID-19 pandemic. Games and Culture, 17(5), 773-794. https://doi.org/10.1177/15554120211056125

Rideout, V., & Robb, M. B. (2019). The Common Sense census: Media use by tweens and teens, 2019. Common Sense Media. https://www.commonsensemedia.org/sites/default/files/research/report/2019-census-8-to-18-full-report-updated.pdf

Scholes, L., Mills, K. A., & Wallace, E. (2021). Boys' gaming identities and opportunities for learning. Learning, Media and Technology, 47(2), 163–178. https://doi.org/10.1080/17439884.2021.1936017

Shoshani, A., & Krauskopf, M. (2021). The Fortnite social paradox: The effects of violent-cooperative multi-player video games on children's basic psychological needs and prosocial behavior. Computers in Human Behavior, 116, 106641. https://doi.org/10.1016/j.chb.2020.106641

Sjöblom, M., Törhönen, M., Hamari, J., & Macey, J. (2019). The ingredients of Twitch streaming: Affordances of game streams. Computers in Human Behavior, 92, 20-28. https://doi.org/10.1016/j.chb.2018.10.012

Smith, A., Toor, S., & Van Kessel, P. (2018). Many turn to YouTube for children's content, news, how-to lessons. Pew Research Center, 7, 1. https://internet.psych.wisc.edu/wp-content/uploads/532-Master/532-UnitPages/Unit-02/Smith_Pew_2018.pdf

Squire, K. (2011). Video games and learning: Teaching and participatory culture in the digital age. Teachers College Press. https://www.researchgate.net/profile/Amy-Lu-8/publication/311654582_Video_Games_and_Learning_Teaching_and_Participatory_Culture_in_the_Digital_Age/links/5b216cb8aca272277fa95dc3/Video-Games-and-Learning-Teaching-and-Participatory-Culture-in-the-Digital-Age.pdf

Steinkuehler, C., & Duncan, S. (2008). Scientific habits of mind in virtual worlds. Journal of Science Education and Technology, 17(6), 530-543. https://doi.org/10.1007/s10956-008-9120-8

Vilasís-Pamos, J., & Pires, F. (2021). How do teens define what it means to be a gamer? Mapping teens' video game practices and cultural imaginaries from a gender and sociocultural perspective.

Information, Communication & Society, 25(12), 1735–1751. https://doi.org/10.1080/1369118X.2021.1883705

Vogels, E. A., Gelles-Watnick, R., & Massarat, N. (2022). Teens, social media and technology 2022. Pew Research Center, 10. https://www.jstor.org/stable/pdf/resrep63507.pdf?acceptTC=true&coverpage=false&addFooter=false

World Health Organization. (2019). International statistical classification of diseases and related health problems (11th ed.). World Health Organization. https://www.who.int/standards/classifications/classification-of-diseases

Chapter 3: Rethinking Success – Skills for a Changing World

Duckworth, A. L., Peterson, C., Matthews, M. D., & Kelly, D. R. (2007). Grit: Perseverance and passion for long-term goals. Journal of Personality and Social Psychology, 92(6), 1087–1101. https://doi.org/10.1037/0022-3514.92.6.1087

Gardner, H. (2011). Frames of mind: The theory of multiple intelligences (3rd ed.). Basic Books. https://books.google.com.ng/books/about/Frames_of_Mind.html?id=wxj6npSaykgC&redir_esc=y

Kohn, A. (2000). The case against standardized testing: Raising the scores, ruining the schools. Heinemann. https://www.heinemann.com/products/e00325.aspx#fulldesc

Robinson, K., & Aronica, L. (2016). Creative schools: The grassroots revolution that's transforming education. Penguin books. https://books.google.com.ng/books/about/Creative_Schools.html?id=4EKLDQAAQBAJ&redir_esc=y

Ryan, R. M., & Deci, E. L. (2000). Self-determination theory and the facilitation of intrinsic motivation, social development, and well-being. American Psychologist, 55(1), 68-78. https://selfdeterminationtheory.org/SDT/documents/2000_RyanDeci_SDT.pdf

Seligman, M. E. (2011). Flourish: A visionary new understanding of happiness and well-being. Simon and Schuster. https://books.google.com.ng/books?hl=en&lr=&id=ng7RJWudoQC&oi=fnd&pg=PA5&dq=Seligman,+M.+E.+P.+(2011).+Flourish:+A+visionary+new+understanding+of+happiness+and+well-being.+Free+Press.&ots=XSQBzPeUPs&sig=MYgQKFD-3oj7Gm1gyhPeJhzliwk&redir_esc=y#v=onepage&q=Seligman%2C%20M.%20E.%20P.%20(2011).%20Flourish%3A%20A%20visionary%20new%20understanding%20of%20happiness%20and%20well-being.%20Free%20Press.&f=false

Wagner, T., & Compton, R. A. (2012). Creating innovators: The making of young people who will change the world. Simon and Schuster. https://books.google.com.ng/books?hl=en&lr=&id=_mp8BgAAQBAJ&oi=fnd&pg=PP9&dq=Wagner,+T.+(2012).+Creating+innovators:+The+making+of+young+people+who+will+change+the+world.+Scribner.&ots=7_eyScpt5J&sig=f51PgqOnhycx7EC6sBdOYFeZjNY&redir_esc=y#v=onepage&q=Wagner%2C%20T.%20(2012).%20Creating%20innovators%3A%20The%20making%20of%20young%20people%20who%20will%20change%20the%20world.%20Scribner.&f=false

PART TWO: UNDERSTOOD

Chapter 4: Building a Growth Mindset in an AI World

Blackwell, L. S., Trzesniewski, K. H., & Dweck, C. S. (2007). Implicit theories of intelligence predict achievement across an adolescent transition: A longitudinal study and an intervention. Child development, 78(1), 246-263. https://doi.org/10.1111/j.1467-8624.2007.00995.x

Doidge, N. (2007). The brain that changes itself: Stories of personal triumph from the frontiers of brain science. Viking. https://psycnet.apa.org/record/2006-23192-000

Dweck, C. S. (2016). Mindset: The new psychology of success (Updated ed.). Random house. https://adrvantage.com/wp-content/uploads/2023/02/Mindset-The-New-Psychology-of-Success-Dweck.pdf

Feldman, R. (2012). Oxytocin and social affiliation in humans. Hormones and behavior, 61(3), 380-391. https://doi.org/10.1016/j.yhbeh.2012.01.008

Haimovitz, K., & Dweck, C. S. (2017). The origins of children's growth and fixed mindsets: New research and a new proposal. Child development, 88(6), 1849-1859. https://doi.org/10.1111/cdev.12955

Szymanska, M., Schneider, M., Chateau-Smith, C., Nezelof, S., & Vulliez-Coady, L. (2017). Psychophysiological effects of oxytocin on parent–child interactions: A literature review on oxytocin and parent–child interactions. Psychiatry and Clinical Neurosciences, 71(10), 690-705. https://doi.org/10.1111/pcn.12544

Moser, J. S., Schroder, H. S., Heeter, C., Moran, T. P., & Lee, Y.-H. (2011). Mind Your Errors: Evidence for a Neural Mechanism Linking Growth Mind-Set to Adaptive Posterior Adjustments. Psychological Science, 22(12), 1484-1489. https://doi.org/10.1177/0956797611419520

Park, D., Gunderson, E. A., Tsukayama, E., Levine, S. C., & Beilock, S. L. (2016). Young children's motivational frameworks and math achievement: Relation to teacher-reported instructional

practices, but not teacher theory of intelligence. Journal of Educational Psychology, 108(3), 300–313.
https://doi.org/10.1037/edu0000064

Rattan, A., Savani, K., Chugh, D., & Dweck, C. S. (2015). Leveraging Mindsets to Promote Academic Achievement: Policy Recommendations. Perspectives on Psychological Science, 10(6), 721-726.
https://doi.org/10.1177/1745691615599383

Rossato, J. I., Bevilaqua, L. R., Izquierdo, I., Medina, J. H., & Cammarota, M. (2009). Dopamine controls persistence of long-term memory storage. Science, 325(5943), 1017-1020.
https://doi.org/10.1126/science.1172545

Yeager, D. S., & Walton, G. M. (2011). Social-Psychological Interventions in Education: They're Not Magic. Review of Educational Research, 81(2), 267-301.
https://doi.org/10.3102/0034654311405999

Zatorre, R. J., Fields, R. D., & Johansen-Berg, H. (2012). Plasticity in gray and white: neuroimaging changes in brain structure during learning. Nature neuroscience, 15(4), 528-536.
https://doi.org/10.1038/nn.3045

Chapter 5: The Parent–Child Learning Partnership

Baumrind, D. (1991). The Influence of Parenting Style on Adolescent Competence and Substance Use. The Journal of Early Adolescence, 11(1), 56-95. https://doi.org/10.1177/0272431691111004

Grolnick, W. S., & Ryan, R. M. (1989). Parent styles associated with children's self-regulation and competence in school. Journal of Educational Psychology, 81(2), 143–154.
https://doi.org/10.1037/0022-0663.81.2.143

Joussemet, M., Landry, R., & Koestner, R. (2008). A self-determination theory perspective on parenting. Canadian Psychology /

Psychologie canadienne, 49(3), 194–200. https://doi.org/10.1037/a0012754

Kohn, A. (2005). Unconditional parenting: Moving from rewards and punishments to love and reason. Simon and Schuster. https://books.google.com.ng/books?hl=en&lr=&id=WiVFGBrhbNMC&oi=fnd&pg=PA1&dq=Kohn,+A.+(2005).+Unconditional+parenting:+Moving+from+rewards+and+punishments+to+love+and+reason.+Atria+Books.&ots=eH7-kwy5mO&sig=5W8MJMdtGxaBKBIu7uHS5WRnJHA&redir_esc=y#v=onepage&q=Kohn%2C%20A.%20(2005).%20Unconditional%20parenting%3A%20Moving%20from%20rewards%20and%20punishments%20to%20love%20and%20reason.%20Atria%20Books.&f=false

Patall, E. A., Cooper, H., & Robinson, J. C. (2008). The effects of choice on intrinsic motivation and related outcomes: A meta-analysis of research findings. Psychological Bulletin, 134(2), 270–300. https://doi.org/10.1037/0033-2909.134.2.270

Ryan, R. M., & Deci, E. L. (2017). Self-determination theory: Basic psychological needs in motivation, development, and wellness. The Guilford Press. https://doi.org/10.1521/978.14625/28806

Siegel, D. J., & Hartzell, M. (2013). Parenting from the inside out: How a deeper self-understanding can help you raise children who thrive. Penguin. https://books.google.com.ng/books/about/Parenting_from_the_Inside_Out.html?id=EGuNEAAAQBAJ&redir_esc=y

Steinberg, L. (2001). We know some things: Parent–adolescent relationships in retrospect and prospect. Journal of research on adolescence, 11(1), 1-19. https://doi.org/10.1111/1532-7795.00001

Chapter 6: Technology and AI in Learning

Yim, I. H. Y. (2024). A critical review of teaching and learning artificial intelligence (AI) literacy: Developing an intelligence-based AI literacy framework for primary school education. Computers and Education: Artificial Intelligence, 7, 100319. https://doi.org/10.1016/j.caeai.2024.100319

Walter, Y. (2024). Embracing the future of Artificial Intelligence in the classroom: the relevance of AI literacy, prompt engineering, and critical thinking in modern education. International Journal of Educational Technology in Higher Education, 21(1), 15. https://doi.org/10.1186/s41239-024-00448-3

Barocas, S., Hardt, M., & Narayanan, A. (2019). Fairness and machine learning: Limitations and opportunities. MIT Press. https://books.google.com.ng/books?hl=en&lr=&id=HuGwE-AAAQBAJ&oi=fnd&pg=PR9&dq=Barocas,+S.,+Hardt,+M.,+%26+Narayanan,+A.+(2019).+Fairness+and+machine+learning:+Limitations+and+opportunities.+MIT+Press.&ots=Q0ggPzf7n8&sig=34ysEH0xpjwuOHPRgCRY7EVJkKM&redir_esc=y#v=onepage&q=Barocas%2C%20S.%2C%20Hardt%2C%20M.%2C%20%26%20Narayanan%2C%20A.%20(2019).%20Fairness%20and%20machine%20learning%3A%20Limitations%20and%20opportunities.%20MIT%20Press.&f=false

Hoffman, M. L. (2000). Empathy and moral development: Implications for caring and justice. Cambridge University Press. https://doi.org/10.1017/CBO9780511805851

Holmes, W., Persson, J., Chounta, I. A., Wasson, B., & Dimitrova, V. (2022). Artificial intelligence and education: A critical view through the lens of human rights, democracy and the rule of law. Council of Europe. https://books.google.com.ng/books?hl=en&lr=&id=RM-lE-AAAQBAJ&oi=fnd&pg=PA5&dq=Holmes,+W.,+Persson,+J.,+Ch

ounta,+I.+A.,+Wasson,+B.,+%26+Dimitrova,+V.+(2024).+Artificial+intelligence+and+education:+A+critical+view+through+the+lens+of+human+rights,+democracy+and+the+rule+of+law.+Council+of+Europe+Publishing.&ots=gdc_Ru_iC3&sig=9jokYpEspWigaBBt4wdgzIiF5Yk&redir_esc=y#v=onepage&q&f=false

Akgun, S., & Greenhow, C. (2022). Artificial intelligence in education: Addressing ethical challenges in K-12 settings. AI and ethics, 2(3), 431–440. https://doi.org/10.1007/s43681-021-00096-7

Long, D., & Magerko, B. (2020). What is AI literacy? Competencies and design considerations. In Proceedings of the 2020 CHI conference on human factors in computing systems (pp. 1-16). https://doi.org/10.1145/3313831.3376727

Noble, S. U. (2018). Algorithms of oppression: How search engines reinforce racism. New York university press. https://doi.org/10.18574/nyu/9781479833641.001.0001

UNESCO, Education Sector. (2019). Artificial intelligence in education: Challenges and opportunities for sustainable development (Working Papers on Education Policy, No. 7). https://www.gcedclearinghouse.org/sites/default/files/resources/190175eng.pdf

Turkle, S. (2011). Alone together: Why we expect more from technology and less from each other. Basic Books. https://www.mediastudies.asia/wp-content/uploads/2017/02/Sherry_Turkle_Alone_Together.pdf

OECD. (2025). Empowering learners for the age of AI: An AI literacy framework for primary and secondary education (Review draft). OECD. https://ailiteracyframework.org/wp-content/uploads/2025/05/AILitFramework_ReviewDraft.pdf

Lang, J. C. (2024). Embracing generative AI for authentic learning. Creative Education, 15(1), 1-20. https://doi.org/10.4236/ce.2024.151001

Winfield, A. F., & Jirotka, M. (2018). Ethical governance is essential to building trust in robotics and artificial intelligence systems. Philosophical Transactions of the Royal Society A: Mathematical, Physical and Engineering Sciences, 376(2133), 20180085. https://doi.org/10.1098/rsta.2018.0085

PART THREE: EQUIPPED

Chapter 7: Beyond the Glass Ceiling — Her Turn

Hupfer, S., Matheson, B., & Crossan, G. (2024). Women and generative AI: The adoption gap is closing fast, but a trust gap persists. Deloitte Insights. https://www.deloitte.com/us/en/insights/industry/technology/technology-media-and-telecom-predictions/2025/women-and-generative-ai.html

Aldasoro, I., Armantier, O., Doerr, S., Gambacorta, L., & Oliviero, T. (2024). The gen AI gender gap. Economics Letters, 241, 111814. https://doi.org/10.1016/j.econlet.2024.111814

Russo, C., Romano, L., Clemente, D., Iacovone, L., Gladwin, T. E., & Panno, A. (2025). Gender differences in artificial intelligence: the role of artificial intelligence anxiety. Frontiers in Psychology, 16, 1559457. https://doi.org/10.3389/fpsyg.2025.1559457

UN Women. (2024). Artificial intelligence and gender equality. United Nations Entity for Gender Equality and the Empowerment of Women. https://www.unwomen.org/en/articles/explainer/artificial-intelligence-and-gender-equality

Willige, A. (2025). Can AI fix the gender gap in STEM? Here's what the data says. World Economic Forum. https://www.weforum.org/stories/2025/03/ai-stem-women-gender-gap/

Chapter 8: What Schools Can (and Can't) Do

American Compass. (2025). Policy brief: Making AI in education work for kids. American Compass. https://americancompass.org/policy-brief-making-ai-in-education-work-for-kids/

Bartlett, S. (Host). (2025). ChatGPT brain rot debate: The fastest way to get dementia, watch this before using ChatGPT again, especially if your kids use it! [Audio podcast episode]. In The Diary of a CEO with Steven Bartlett. Spotify. https://open.spotify.com/episode/5ta3o58Acn70Pj3xU5Exca

AI for Education. (2025). State AI guidance for K12 schools. https://www.aiforeducation.io/ai-resources/state-ai-guidance

National Education Association. (2024). Teaching in the age of AI: NEA members' roadmap for safe, effective, and accessible use of artificial intelligence in education. NEA Today. https://www.nea.org/nea-today/all-news-articles/teaching-age-ai

Policy Analysis for California Education. (2023). AI policy guidance for schools: TeachAI toolkit. https://edpolicyinca.org/publications/ai-policy-guidance-schools

U.S. Department of Education. (2025). Dear colleague letter: Leveraging federal grant funds to improve education outcomes through artificial intelligence . AALRR. https://www.aalrr.com/newsroom-alerts-4159

Miao, F., Holmes, W., Huang, R., & Zhang, H. (2021). AI and education: Guidance for policy-makers. UNESCO. https://www.unesco.org/en/articles/ai-and-education-guidance-policy-makers

White House. (2025, April 23). Executive Order: Advancing artificial intelligence education for American youth.

https://www.whitehouse.gov/presidential-actions/2025/04/advancing-artificial-intelligence-education-for-american-youth/

Chapter 9: Student Voice in the Age of GenAI

Munoz-Najar, A., Bertrand, M., Molina, E., & Cobo, C. (2024). 100 student voices on AI and education. World Bank Blogs. https://blogs.worldbank.org/en/education/100-student-voices-on-ai-and-education

EMMERSON, D. (2025). The importance of student voice in getting AI right for schools. Impact (2514-6955), p. 76. https://openurl.ebsco.com/EPDB%3Agcd%3A1%3A28436417/detailv2?sid=ebsco%3Aplink%3Ascholar&id=ebsco%3Agcd%3A187009520&crl=c&link_origin=scholar.google.com

Chang, M. A., Tissenbaum, M., Philip, T. M., & D'Mello, S. K. (2025). Co-designing AI with youth partners: Enabling ideal classroom relationships through a novel AI relational privacy ethical framework. Computers and Education: Artificial Intelligence, 8, 100364. https://doi.org/10.1016/j.caeai.2025.100364

Cai, Z., Han, A., Zhou, X., Gazulla, E. D., & Peppler, K. (2025). Child-AI Co-Creation: A Review of the Current Research Landscape and a Proposal for Six Design Considerations. Proceedings of the 24th Interaction Design and Children, 916-922. https://doi.org/10.1145/3713043.3731506

UNESCO. (2025). Youth voices shape dialogue and discourse on AI and education and learning practices in Southern Africa. UNESCO Regional Office for Southern Africa. https://www.unesco.org/en/articles/youth-voices-shape-dialogue-and-discourse-ai-and-education-and-learning-practices-southern-africa

Chapter 10: The Power of Play and Creativity

Brown, S., & Vaughan, C. (2009). Play: How it shapes the brain, opens the imagination, and invigorates the soul. Avery/Penguin Group USA. https://psycnet.apa.org/record/2009-17682-000

Gray, P. (2013). Free to learn: Why unleashing the instinct to play will make our children happier, more self-reliant, and better students for life. Basic Books/Hachette Book Group. https://psycnet.apa.org/record/2012-32884-000

Hirsh-Pasek, K., Golinkoff, R. M., Berk, L. E., & Singer, D. G. (2009). A mandate for playful learning in preschool: Presenting the evidence. Oxford University Press. https://books.google.com.ng/books?hl=en&lr=&id=p6sRDAAAQBAJ&oi=fnd&pg=PP1&dq=Hirsh-Pasek,+K.,+Golinkoff,+R.+M.,+Berk,+L.+E.,+%26+Singer,+D.+G.+(2009).+A+mandate+for+playful+learning+in+preschool:+Presenting+the+evidence.+Oxford+University+Press.&ots=-SQW-55BWr&sig=a2pX_bHeZZeVCEajdi3AJ02wqDA&redir_esc=y#v=onepage&q&f=false

Lillard, A. S., Lerner, M. D., Hopkins, E. J., Dore, R. A., Smith, E. D., & Palmquist, C. M. (2013). The impact of pretend play on children's development: A review of the evidence. Psychological Bulletin, 139(1), 1–34. https://doi.org/10.1037/a0029321

Pellegrini, A. D., & Smith, P. K. (1998). Physical activity play: the nature and function of a neglected aspect of playing. Child development, 69(3), 577–598. https://doi.org/10.1111/j.1467-8624.1998.tb06226.x

Russ, S. W., & Dillon, J. A. (2011). Changes in children's pretend play over two decades. Creativity Research Journal, 23(4), 330–338. https://doi.org/10.1080/10400419.2011.621824

Singer, D. G., Golinkoff, R. M., & Hirsh-Pasek, K. (Eds.). (2006). Play = learning: How play motivates and enhances children's cognitive and social-emotional growth. Oxford University Press. https://doi.org/10.1093/acprof:oso/9780195304381.001.0001

Vygotsky, L. S. (1978). Mind in society: The development of higher psychological processes. Harvard University Press. https://books.google.com.ng/books?hl=en&lr=&id=RxjjUefze_oC&oi=fnd&pg=PA1&dq=Vygotsky,+L.+S.+(1978).+Mind+in+society:+The+development+of+higher+psychological+processes.+Harvard+University+Press.&ots=okA1PYm18u&sig=Jhg2LU_n-L5h7lEVA9bCNKymTHA&redir_esc=y#v=onepage&q=Vygotsky%2C%20L.%20S.%20(1978).%20Mind%20in%20society%3A%20The%20development%20of%20higher%20psychological%20processes.%20Harvard%20University%20Press.&f=false

Chapter 11: Raising Independent Learners

Deci, E. L., & Ryan, R. M. (2000). The "what" and "why" of goal pursuits: Human needs and the self-determination of behavior. Psychological Inquiry, 11(4), 227–268. https://doi.org/10.1207/S15327965PLI1104_01

Gray, P. (2011). The decline of play and the rise of psychopathology in children and adolescents. American Journal of Play, 3(4), 443–463. https://files.eric.ed.gov/fulltext/EJ985541.pdf

Grolnick, W. S., Deci, E. L., & Ryan, R. M. (1997). Internalization within the family: The self-determination theory perspective. In J. E. Grusec & L. Kuczynski (Eds.), Parenting and children's internalization of values: A handbook of contemporary theory (pp. 135–161). John Wiley & Sons Inc. https://selfdeterminationtheory.org/wp-content/uploads/2020/10/1997_GrolnickDeciRyan.pdf

Hansen Sandseter, E. B. (2007). Categorising risky play — how can we identify risk-taking in children's play? European Early Childhood Education Research Journal, 15(2), 237–252.
https://doi.org/10.1080/13502930701321733

Skenazy, L. (2021). Free-range kids: how parents and teachers can let go and let grow. John Wiley & Sons.
https://www.wiley.com/en-ie/Free-Range+Kids%3A+How+Parents+and+Teachers+Can+Let+Go+and+Let+Grow%2C+2nd+Edition-p-9781119782148

Soenens, B., & Vansteenkiste, M. (2010). A theoretical upgrade of the concept of parental psychological control: Proposing new insights on the basis of self-determination theory. Developmental Review, 30(1), 74–99. https://doi.org/10.1016/j.dr.2009.11.001

Steinberg L. (2013). The influence of neuroscience on US Supreme Court decisions about adolescents' criminal culpability. Nature reviews. Neuroscience, 14(7), 513–518.
https://doi.org/10.1038/nrn3509

Wood, D., Bruner, J. S., & Ross, G. (1976). The role of tutoring in problem solving. Child Psychology & Psychiatry & Allied Disciplines, 17(2), 89–100. https://doi.org/10.1111/j.1469-7610.1976.tb00381.x

Chapter 12: The Art of Letting Go

Clark, A., & Chalmers, D. (1998). The extended mind. analysis, 58(1), 7-19. https://www.alice.id.tue.nl/references/clark-chalmers-1998.pdf

Gelles, D. (2015). Mindful work: How meditation is changing business from the inside out. Houghton Mifflin Harcourt.
https://books.google.com.ng/books?hl=en&lr=&id=rxC9BgAAQ

BAJ&oi=fnd&pg=PP1&dq=Gelles,+D.+(2015).+Mindful+work:+How+meditation+is+changing+business+from+the+inside+out.+Houghton+Mifflin+Harcourt.&ots=jE6RLcGazy&sig=-0S8pJ86PLEQG24px5DPLqfJl0Y&redir_esc=y#v=onepage&q=Gelles%2C%20D.%20(2015).%20Mindful%20work%3A%20How%20meditation%20is%20changing%20business%20from%20the%20inside%20out.%20Houghton%20Mifflin%20Harcourt.&f=false

Skerrett, P. J. (2012). Multitasking: A medical and mental hazard. Harvard Health Publishing. https://www.health.harvard.edu/blog/multitasking-a-medical-and-mental-hazard-201201074063

Hiniker, A., Schoenebeck, S. Y., & Kientz, J. A. (2016). Not at the dinner table: Parents' and children's perspectives on family technology rules. In Proceedings of the 19th ACM conference on computer-supported cooperative work & social computing (pp. 1376-1389). https://doi.org/10.1145/2818048.2819940

Kabat-Zinn, M., & Kabat-Zinn, J. (1997). Everyday blessings: The inner work of mindful parenting. Hyperion. https://inquiringmind.com/article/1401_26_kabat-zinn_review_alexander/

Radesky, J. S., & Christakis, D. A. (2016). Increased Screen Time: Implications for Early Childhood Development and Behavior. Pediatric clinics of North America, 63(5), 827–839. https://doi.org/10.1016/j.pcl.2016.06.006

Reed, J., Hirsh-Pasek, K., & Golinkoff, R. M. (2017). Learning on hold: Cell phones sidetrack parent-child interactions. Developmental psychology, 53(8), 1428–1436. https://doi.org/10.1037/dev0000292

Turkle, S. (2015). Reclaiming conversation: The power of talk in a digital age. Penguin. https://e-edu.nbu.bg/pluginfile.php/849202/mod_resource/content/1/Sherry-Turkle%20-%20Reclaiming%20Conversation%20-%20The%20Power%20of%20Talk%20in%20a%20Digital%20Age%202015.pdf

Zimmerman, F. J., Christakis, D. A., & Meltzoff, A. N. (2007). Associations between media viewing and language development in children under age 2 years. The Journal of pediatrics, 151(4), 364–368. https://doi.org/10.1016/j.jpeds.2007.04.071

Chapter 13: Guardrails not Gatekeepers

Alloway, T. P. (2013). Working memory: The connected intelligence. Routledge. https://www.routledge.com/Working-Memory-The-Connected-Intelligence/Alloway/p/book/9781848726185?srsltid=AfmBOoof95Y4r_jRI9YAYDhCxku575pUEj31_0hHD2HZFlRg4K5JFIoi

Bandura, A. (2006). Guide for constructing self-efficacy scales. In F. Pajares & T. Urdan (Eds.), Self-efficacy beliefs of adolescents, 5(1), 307-337. Information Age Publishing. https://books.google.com.ng/books?hl=en&lr=&id=P_onDwAAQBAJ&oi=fnd&pg=PA307&dq=Bandura,+A.+(2006).+Guide+for+constructing+self-efficacy+scales.+In+F.+Pajares+%26+T.+Urdan+(Eds.),+Self-efficacy+beliefs+of+adolescents+(pp.+307-337).+Information+Age+Publishing.&ots=rkNNp-EmAS&sig=eL6uoKyYT8MgRYT3KLWmHr1tvko&redir_esc=y#v=onepage&q&f=false

Freire, P. (1970). Pedagogy of the Oppressed. Continuum Books. https://books.google.com.ng/books/about/Pedagogy_of_the_Oppressed.html?id=M4MQAAAAYAAJ&redir_esc=y

Grinspoon, P. J. (2020). The health effects of too much gaming. Harvard Health Publishing. https://www.health.harvard.edu/blog/the-health-effects-of-too-much-gaming-2020122221645

Palmer, P. J. (2007). The courage to teach: exploring the inner landscape of a teacher's life. 10th anniversary ed. Jossey-Bass. https://cmc.marmot.org/Record/.b33484351

Prensky, M. (2010). Teaching digital natives: Partnering for real learning. Corwin Press. https://www.corwin.com/books/teaching-digital-natives-233944?srsltid=AfmBOorp3z-dOAz97CRK-TiCVNH1pYqu6nKTHbXAJPcZkIHa6AB3khR6j

Sinek, S. (2009). Start with why: How great leaders inspire everyone to take action. Portfolio. https://www.earthgifts.com.au/ebook/simon-sinek-start-with-why.pdf?srsltid=AfmBOopbCQNohkfof99A77QfFDqfs1eRpih-iTCAugXEcZFu1gnb3QFa

PART FOUR: DIFFERENT MINDS, SAME FUTURE

Chapter 14: Wired Differently – AI and Children with Learning Differences

American Psychiatric Association. (2013). Diagnostic and statistical manual of mental disorders: DSM-5 (5th ed.). American Psychiatric Publishing.
https://doi.org/10.1176/appi.books.9780890425596

Attwood, A. (2006). The complete guide to Asperger's syndrome. Jessica Kingsley Publishers. https://www.autismforthvalley.co.uk/files/5314/4595/7798/Attwood-Tony-The-Complete-Guide-to-Aspergers-Syndrome.pdf

Baum, S.M., Schader, R.M., & Owen, S.V. (2017). To Be Gifted and Learning Disabled: Strength-Based Strategies for Helping Twice-

Exceptional Students With LD, ADHD, ASD, and More (3rd ed.). Routledge. https://www.routledge.com/To-Be-Gifted-and-Learning-Disabled-Strength-Based-Strategies-for-Helping-Twice-Exceptional-Students-With-LD-ADHD-ASD-and-More/Baum-Schader-Owen/p/book/9781618216441?srsltid=Afm-BOoqw3D07EZHC8ZAlOQ_XoHzpF7ttiUMAL-RyLOY7f6J_Xy3JKlDZx

Grynszpan, O., Weiss, P. L., Perez-Diaz, F., & Gal, E. (2014). Innovative technology-based interventions for autism spectrum disorders: a meta-analysis. Autism : the international journal of research and practice, 18(4), 346–361.
https://doi.org/10.1177/1362361313476767

Smith, I. (2017). Multisensory approaches to learning. In Disability and Inclusion in Early Years Education (pp. 140-161). Routledge. https://www.taylorfrancis.com/chapters/edit/10.4324/9781315637877-8/multisensory-approaches-learning-ingrid-smith

Knight, V., McKissick, B. R., & Saunders, A. (2013). A review of technology-based interventions to teach academic skills to students with autism spectrum disorder. Journal of autism and developmental disorders, 43(11), 2628–2648.
https://doi.org/10.1007/s10803-013-1814-y

Ringland, K. E., Wolf, C. T., Boyd, L. E., Baldwin, M. S., & Hayes, G. R. (2016, October). Would you be mine: Appropriating minecraft as an assistive technology for youth with autism. In Proceedings of the 18th International ACM SIGACCESS Conference on Computers and Accessibility (pp. 33-41).
https://doi.org/10.1145/2982142.2982172

Ringland, K. E., Wolf, C. T., Faucett, H., Dombrowski, L., & Hayes, G. R. (2016, May). " Will I always be not social?" Re-

Conceptualizing Sociality in the Context of a Minecraft Community for Autism. In Proceedings of the 2016 CHI conference on human factors in computing systems (pp. 1256-1269). https://doi.org/10.1145/2858036.285803

Rose, D. H., & Meyer, A. (2002). Teaching every student in the digital age: Universal design for learning. Association for Supervision and Curriculum Development. https://books.google.com.ng/books/about/Teaching_Every_Student_in_the_Digital_Ag.html?id=_B0iAQAAIAAJ&redir_esc=y

Thomas-Hughes, H., Barke, J., & Clayton, A. (2025). Working With Students as Co-Researchers; a Reflection on Process. Journal of Participatory Research Methods, 6(2), 310-317. https://jprm.scholasticahq.com/article/129350.pdf

Chapter 15: High-Voltage Hearts, High Speed Minds – Supporting Gifted Kids with AI

Dai, D. Y. (2010). The nature and nurture of giftedness: A new framework for understanding gifted education. Teachers College Press. https://psycnet.apa.org/record/2010-14823-000

Davis, G. A., Rimm, S. B., & Siegle, D. (2011). Education of the gifted and talented (6th ed.). Pearson. https://api.pageplace.de/preview/DT0400.9781292035130_A24589390/preview-9781292035130_A24589390.pdf

Grugan, M. C., Olsson, L. F., Hill, A. P., & Madigan, D. J. (2025). Perfectionism, School Burnout, and School Engagement in Gifted Students: The Role of Stress. Gifted Child Quarterly, 69(3), 255-268. https://doi.org/10.1177/00169862251328015

Kanevsky, L., & Keighley, T. (2003). To produce or not to produce? Understanding boredom and the honor in underachievement. Roeper Review, 26(1), 20-28.

https://doi.org/10.1080/02783190309554235Renzulli, J. S. (2012). Reexamining the role of gifted education and talent development for the 21st century: A four-part theoretical approach. Gifted Child Quarterly, 56(3), 150–159. https://doi.org/10.1177/0016986212444901

Robinson, A., Shore, B. M., & Enersen, D. (2021). Best practices in gifted education: An evidence-based guide. Routledge. https://doi.org/10.4324/9781003233244Subotnik, R. F., Olszewski-Kubilius, P., & Worrell, F. C. (2011). Rethinking Giftedness and Gifted Education: A Proposed Direction Forward Based on Psychological Science. Psychological Science in the Public Interest, 12(1), 3-54. https://doi.org/10.1177/1529100611418056

Winner, E. (1996). Gifted children: Myths and realities. Basic Books. https://psycnet.apa.org/record/1996-97810-000

PART FIVE: TAKING ACTION

Chapter 16: Empowering Your Home with AI

Clark, A., & Chalmers, D. (1998). The extended mind. analysis, 58(1), 7-19. https://www.jstor.org/stable/3328150

Gelles, D. (2015). Mindful work: How meditation is changing business from the inside out. Houghton Mifflin Harcourt. https://books.google.com.ng/books?hl=en&lr=&id=rxC9BgAAQBAJ&oi=fnd&pg=PP1&dq=Gelles,+D.+(2015).+Mindful+work:+How+meditation+is+changing+business+from+the+inside+out.+Houghton+Mifflin+Harcourt.&ots=jE6RLdFiAy&sig=5TzdfsidG5hoM9XrP4NhfT9FQ9c&redir_esc=y#v=onepage&q=Gelles%2C%20D.%20(2015).%20Mindful%20work%3A%20How%20meditation%20is%20changing%20business%20from%20the%20inside%20out.%20Houghton%20Mifflin%20Harcourt.&f=false

Hiniker, A., Schoenebeck, S. Y., & Kientz, J. A. (2016, February). Not at the dinner table: Parents' and children's perspectives on family technology rules. In Proceedings of the 19th ACM conference on computer-supported cooperative work & social computing (pp. 1376-1389). https://doi.org/10.1145/2818048.281994

Kabat-Zinn, M., & Kabat-Zinn, J. (1997). Everyday blessings: The inner work of mindful parenting. Hyperion. https://inquiringmind.com/article/1401_26_kabat-zinn_review_alexander/

Radesky, J. S., & Christakis, D. A. (2016). Increased Screen Time: Implications for Early Childhood Development and Behavior. Pediatric clinics of North America, 63(5), 827–839. https://doi.org/10.1016/j.pcl.2016.06.006

Reed, J., Hirsh-Pasek, K., & Golinkoff, R. M. (2017). Learning on hold: Cell phones sidetrack parent-child interactions. Developmental psychology, 53(8), 1428–1436. https://doi.org/10.1037/dev0000292

Sherry, T. (2015). Reclaiming conversation: The power of talk in a digital age. Penguin Press. https://e-edu.nbu.bg/pluginfile.php/849202/mod_resource/content/1/Sherry-Turkle%20-%20Reclaiming%20Conversation%20-%20The%20Power%20of%20Talk%20in%20a%20Digital%20Age%202015.pdf

Zimmerman, F. J., Christakis, D. A., & Meltzoff, A. N. (2007). Associations between media viewing and language development in children under age 2 years. The Journal of pediatrics, 151(4), 364–368. https://doi.org/10.1016/j.jpeds.2007.04.071

Chapter 17: Navigating the Future Together

Bandura, A. (2006). Guide for Constructing Self-Efficacy Scales. In F. Pajares, & T. C. Urdan (Eds.), Self-Efficacy Beliefs of

Adolescents (pp. 307-337). IAP Information Age Publishing. https://books.google.com.ng/books?hl=en&lr=&id=P_onDwAAQBAJ&oi=fnd&pg=PA307&dq=Bandura,+A.+(2006).+Guide+for+constructing+self-efficacy+scales.+In+F.+Pajares+%26+T.+Urdan+(Eds.),+Self-efficacy+beliefs+of+adolescents+(pp.+307-337).+Information+Age+Publishing.&ots=rkNNp0DjBL&sig=HWJk6SHfzbN5u1sl1pZIje1bubY&redir_esc=y#v=onepage&q&f=false

Dweck, C. S. (2016). Mindset: The new psychology of success (Updated ed.). Ballantine Books. https://adrvantage.com/wp-content/uploads/2023/02/Mindset-The-New-Psychology-of-Success-Dweck.pdf

Freire, P. (1970). Pedagogy of the oppressed. Continuum International Publishing Group. https://books.google.com.ng/books/about/Pedagogy_of_the_Oppressed.html?id=M4MQAAAAYAAJ&redir_esc=y

Palmer, P. J. (2007). The courage to teach: Exploring the inner landscape of a teacher's life (10th anniversary ed.). Jossey-Bass. https://www.abebooks.com/9780787996864/Courage-Teach-Exploring-Landscape-Teachers-0787996866/plp

Prensky, M. (2010). Teaching digital natives: Partnering for real learning. Corwin Press. https://books.google.com.ng/books?hl=en&lr=&id=3JhE_QIjfagC&oi=fnd&pg=PP1&dq=Prensky,+M.+(2010).+Teaching+digital+natives:+Partnering+for+real+learning.+Corwin+Press.&ots=6n8gByvLYu&sig=npbFmADsq-MmhiNxe303mmswOs&redir_esc=y#v=onepage&q=Prensky%2C%20M.%20(2010).%20Teaching%20digital%20natives%3A%20Partnering%20for%20real%20learning.%20Corwin%20Press.&f=false

Sinek, S. (2009). Start with why: How great leaders inspire everyone to take action. Portfolio. https://www.earthgifts.com.au/ebook/simon-sinek-start-with-why.pdf?srsltid=AfmBOoowPcPJgun-JILDbmOSYT0uUkLv_OFx_I8y1nLipAGIfJs4Ysw1O

Vygotsky, L. S. (1978). Mind in society: The development of higher psychological processes. Harvard University Press. https://books.google.com.ng/books?hl=en&lr=&id=RxjjUefze_oC&oi=fnd&pg=PA1&dq=Vygotsky,+L.+S.+(1978).+Mind+in+society:+The+development+of+higher+psychological+processes.+Harvard+University+Press.&ots=okA1PZp2fp&sig=468A4HoLF_Nmusn8mZSOaIqw00o&redir_esc=y#v=onepage&q=Vygotsky%2C%20L.%20S.%20(1978).%20Mind%20in%20society%3A%20The%20development%20of%20higher%20psychological%20processes.%20Harvard%20University%20Press.&f=false

Further Reading / Grey Literature

Brown University Health. (n.d.). *Multitasking and how it affects your brain health.* https://www.brownhealth.org/be-well/multitasking-and-how-it-affects-your-brain-health

Fishman, A. (2021). Women in gaming: A difficult intersection. *Psychology Today.* https://www.psychologytoday.com/us/blog/video-game-health/202201/women-

Johnson, S. B. (2023). Kids and video games: The good and the bad. *Akron Children's Hospital Blog.* https://www.akronchildrens.org/inside/2023/02/13/kids-and-video-games-the-good-and-the-bad

WellPower. (2023). The surprising truth about video games and mental health. https://www.wellpower.org/blog/the-surprising-truth-about-video-games-and-mental-health

Livingstone, S., & Pothong, K. (2022). How does *Playful by Design* work in practice? The case of Fortnite. *Parenting for a Digital Future Blog.*

https://blogs.lse.ac.uk/parenting4digitalfuture/2022/03/30/playful-by-design-fortnite/

EPILOGUE:
A LEGACY OF CURIOSITY

This book is a product of my life's work—as a parent, as a teacher, and as a HALT-accredited educator committed to preparing young people for the world ahead.

I am quietly energised by the pace of change, because I believe it is always going to take something of this scale—something like AI—to pull education forward. For more than a century, classrooms have followed the same formula: students seated in rows, facing a board—blackboards became whiteboards, chalk became markers, but the core model barely shifted.

Now, everything is shifting.

But parents and teachers don't need to be afraid.

In my classroom, I'm witnessing something powerful. I'm watching students light up—not because AI replaces them, but because it reveals them. It helps them find the words, the confidence, the clarity they didn't know they had. I've watched my own son walk away from a system that couldn't see him, only to create a life that finally does. I've seen parents cry in gratitude when, for the first time, their child found their voice through a project powered by technology.

This isn't just a technological shift — it's a human one.

We are not raising robots.

We are raising readers of nuance, writers of their futures, and thinkers who will navigate what we cannot yet predict.

If you take one thing from this book, let it be this:

Your child doesn't need to be protected from the future.

They need to be prepared for it — ethically, creatively, and lovingly.

Trust their capacity to adapt.

Trust your role as their anchor.

And trust that technology, when guided well, can help us raise not just smarter children, but kinder ones too.

There's no single path anymore. Learning is a climb with many routes — and nobody goes alone. Teachers, parents, grandparents, carers and fellow students lift each other as every child finds the path that fits them best.

A NOTE TO PARENTS

Thank you for walking through this book with us. Writing it has been our first attempt at authorship—a leap into unknown territory. We know some of what we've written may feel controversial, and no doubt there will be critics. But isn't that exactly what we encourage our children to do? To have a go. To step out. To try, even when it's uncomfortable.

In our home, we've often said: "Don't care what they think—just give it your best." That's what we've done here. And we wonder—when was the last time you really put yourself out there, risked being seen, and tried something bold?

AI is perhaps the most seismic shift in education we have ever witnessed. It can feel overwhelming, but it doesn't have to. You don't need to be an expert to guide your child. You just need to stay curious, keep asking questions, and walk alongside them as they navigate this new world.

AI will change how they learn, work, and create — but it will never replace the values, resilience, and belonging that you give them. That's your enduring gift as a parent.

This book has been our attempt to model exactly what we ask of our kids: to learn, to grow, and to be brave enough to contribute to the conversation. Our hope is that it gives you courage too — not just to face the future, but to shape it with your children.

With gratitude and hope,

Vanessa and Darren

To my fellow educators —

Don't bury your heads in the sand. Artificial intelligence may feel overwhelming, even unsettling at times, but you are still at the heart of learning. Decades from now, when our students look back, they will not remember the tool or the technology that shaped them most. They will remember you. Your encouragement, your belief in them, your ability to see what others couldn't.

Teaching has always been a gift and a privilege. Artificial intelligence does not take that away. If anything, it frees us to lean into what only humans can do — connect, inspire, challenge, and care. You are still some of the most memorable people in these students' lives, and no algorithm can replace the imprint of a great teacher.

The temptation in times of change is to retreat, to hold on tightly to what we know. But this is not a time to fear — it is a time to step forward with courage. Artificial intelligence will change how we teach, but it will never diminish why we teach.

This book has been written for parents. But my next one will be written for you — teachers on the frontline — so that you feel supported, resourced, and energised for the seismic shift we're living through. Because the truth is this: education has never mattered more. And neither have you.

With deep respect,

Vanessa

ACKNOWLEDGEMENTS

To Darren—

Your deep passion for the human brain, for healing, and for the incredible potential within people has been the steady foundation of this book. Thank you for the way you've poured your knowledge into our conversations, grounding vision with science, and for the way you love our family so fiercely. This book carries your fingerprints as much as mine.

To my children—

You teach me more than I could ever hope to teach you. Your curiosity, courage, frustrations, and triumphs remind me daily of why this work matters. You are both the inspiration and the compass that keep me moving forward.

To my colleagues—

You have shaped my career in ways I will never forget. Every conversation, every challenge, every shared victory has contributed to the teacher and leader I have become. I am deeply grateful for the wisdom, camaraderie, and shared purpose we hold in the vocation of education.

And to every reader —

This book is for you. Thank you for walking with me into this unknown, urgent, and hope-filled future.

www.ingramcontent.com/pod-product-compliance
Lightning Source LLC
Chambersburg PA
CBHW031418150426
43191CB00006B/315